BRAIN-STRETCHING
LOGIC
PUZZLES

LARRY R. CLARKE

PUZZLE
WRIGHT
PRESS

New York

PUZZLE WRIGHT PRESS
New York

An Imprint of Sterling Publishing
1166 Avenue of the Americas
New York, NY 10036

ISBN 978-1-4549-3036-5

Distributed in Canada by Sterling Publishing Co., Inc.
℅ Canadian Manda Group, 664 Annette Street
Toronto, Ontario M6S 2C8, Canada
Distributed in the United Kingdom by GMC Distribution Services
Castle Place, 166 High Street, Lewes, East Sussex BN7 1XU, England
Distributed in Australia by NewSouth Books
University of New South Wales, Sydney, NSW 2052, Australia

For information about custom editions, special sales, and premium
and corporate purchases, please contact Sterling Special Sales at
800-805-5489 or specialsales@sterlingpublishing.com.

Manufactured in Canada

2 4 6 8 10 9 7 5 3 1

sterlingpublishing.com
puzzlewright.com

Cover design by Valerie Hou
Front cover image by _human/iStock
Interior illustrations by Rob Collinet

Contents

Introduction

This is the fourth in my series of logic puzzle books, the previous collections being *Challenging Logic Puzzles* (which has sold over 90,000 copies), *Extreme Logic Puzzles*, and *Supergenius Logic Puzzles*, all of which feature a variety of visual and logical brainteasers. My puzzle columns in the U.K.'s *Prospect* magazine and *The Daily Telegraph* have undeniably provided the inspiration for many of these enigmas, but almost all of the problems here are entirely new.

For those with a finely tuned mind, this book will certainly let you exercise it. For those who want to improve at solving logic puzzles, some of the problem types are repeated to give the solver a chance to become familiar with the method of approach.

The puzzles presented here gradually increase in difficulty as the book progresses. The answers are given in the back of the book, but not in order. (It would be an unwelcome frustration to see the answer to the next puzzle before attempting it.)

So find a silent place where you can listen to your inner inspiration, and celebrate your eventual success!

—Barry R. Clarke
Oxford
barryispuzzled.com

Four Aces

At the Card Conundrum Club, four aces are placed on the table in a row without any other club member seeing them. They are then rearranged into the order shown. Three facts are true about the original order:

1) The spade was somewhere to the left of the club.
2) Exactly one card has not moved from its original position.
3) The diamond was not next to the heart.

Can you deduce the original order of the cards?

Solution on page 94.

Psychic Sid

The latest prediction from Psychic Sid is that on one day next week it will snow ... he just can't seem to decide which. He has made four attempts at a prediction:

Attempt 1: "Tuesday, Thursday, Friday, or Sunday."
Attempt 2: "Monday, Tuesday, Wednesday, or Saturday."
Attempt 3: "Monday, Tuesday, Thursday, or Sunday."
Attempt 4: "Monday, Wednesday, Friday, or Sunday."

We looked into the future and learned that only one of Sid's attempted predictions is accurate. On what day will it snow?

Solution on page 69.

Digital Deletions 1

$$
\begin{array}{r}
3\ 4\ 6\ 8 \\
+\ 3\ 7\ 2\ 8 \\
\hline
7\ 1\ 9\ 6
\end{array}
$$

In the addition problem above, delete one digit from each row (closing up the gaps in each case) to leave three columns of digits that still form a correct sum. Then repeat the process, erasing a second digit from each row to leave two columns, and finally a third to leave one column, closing the gaps to leave a correct sum after each deletion as before. Which numbers should be deleted and in what order?

Solution on page 60.

Salt and Pepper

Antwit, Babble, and Crumble are eating lunch at a round table. Their seating arrangement is in that order when viewed counterclockwise from above. One of them has the salt shaker, another has the pepper grinder, and the third has neither.

Antwit says, "The person to my left has the salt."
Babble says, "The person to my right has the pepper."
Crumble says, "Taken together, I and the person to my left have only the salt."

All three are lying. Who has the salt and who has the pepper?

Solution on page 70.

The Solar Society 1

At the January meeting of the Solar Society, the six members who attend (including Ms. Neptune) sit in a circle on six equally spaced chairs (numbered as shown above) facing the image of the Sun on the tiled floor. The group leader for the month sits in chair 1. At no time does more than one person occupy a chair. Their positions in the circle are as follows:

1) Mr. Jupiter does not sit next to Mr. Uranus.
2) Mr. Mercury, who is not January's group leader, sits to the immediate right of Ms. Saturn, who is not opposite the group leader.
3) Ms. Venus sits two places to the right of Mr. Jupiter.
4) Mr. Uranus sits at least two places from January's group leader.

Can you deduce the seating arrangement?

Solution on page 61.

Pieces of Eight

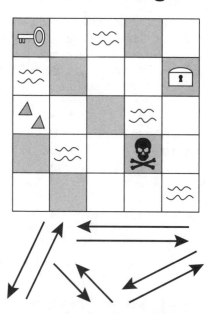

Above is Pirate Pete's treasure map. The dark squares represent islands and the light squares represent water. Starting at the skull and crossbones, place all eight arrows on the grid without changing their orientation so that each connects the centers of two islands. Every island must be visited in a closed circuit, and the key must be acquired before reaching the treasure chest. Under no circumstances may the shark-infested water (square with gray triangles) be crossed by any part of any arrow! Can you place the eight arrows correctly on the grid?

Solution on page 64.

Clues and Queues

Antwit, Babble, Crumble, Dibdib, Earwig, and Fritter are queueing for tickets at the Gibbon Theater. A new play is being performed that evening starring that great actor Larry Olive-Hair and the demand is high. Time passes and the six friends soon find themselves occupying the front six positions in the queue. The following facts are true about their order in the line:

1) Antwit is not next to Crumble or Dibdib.
2) Babble is two places from Crumble.
3) Dibdib is three places from Earwig.
4) Fritter is two places behind Earwig.

Can you give the order in which they're standing in the queue, from front to back?

Solution on page 67.

The Four Chairs

Antwit	Babble
Crumble	Dibdib

Four friends, Antwit, Babble, Crumble, and Dibdib, sit in a 2×2 arrangement of chairs in the positions shown above. A dispute breaks out and they decide to rearrange themselves, one to a chair, so that no person occupies their original position. The following conditions apply to their new positions:

1) Antwit is somewhere in the row below Babble.
2) Crumble is in an adjacent column to Dibdib.

What is their new seating arrangement?

Solution on page 69.

Digital Deletions 2

$$
\begin{array}{r}
8\ 2\ 9\ 7 \\
-\ 3\ 7\ 2\ 8 \\
\hline
4\ 5\ 6\ 9
\end{array}
$$

In the subtraction problem above, delete one digit from each row (closing up the gaps in each case) to leave three columns of digits that still form a correct subtraction problem. Then repeat the process, erasing a second digit from each row to leave two columns, and finally a third to leave one column, closing the gaps to leave a correct subtraction after each deletion as before. Which numbers should be deleted and in what order?

Solution on page 63.

Lousy Electrics 1

An apartment has four rooms: downstairs, a dining room and kitchen; and upstairs, a bathroom and bedroom. In each room is a light switch and a light fixture, but the electrical wiring has been incorrectly installed. Only one of the four light switches controls the light fixture in the same room. For the other three rooms, each switch activates a light in a different room (there being only one switch connected to each light).

1) The kitchen light is not activated by the switch in either the kitchen or the bathroom.
2) The dining room switch is connected to one of the upstairs lights.

Can you determine which switches control which lights?

Solution on page 72.

Presto!

As the Amazing Presto stands in front of his audience, he places four top hats (labeled A–D from left to right) in a line on the table before them, with the open ends facing up.

"And now," says Presto, "I shall produce a rabbit from the first hat."

Suddenly, an elf pops up from inside hat A and says, "It's in one of the middle two."

The show must go on, so Presto ignores him, and as he is about to plunge his hand into hat B, an elf jumps up from that hat and announces, "It's now in one of the two on the ends."

Before Presto can react, an elf in hat C declares, "It's moved again—now it's in B or D."

Finally, from hat D an elf says, "Not quick enough, Presto! It's now in hat A or C."

Presto gives up, and is informed by his assistant (also an elf) that the rabbit has visited each hat exactly once in some order, and in at least one instance it was occupying a hat that wasn't adjacent to the one from which the elf was speaking.

In what order did the rabbit inhabit the hats?

Solution on page 94.

Cake Mix

	First name	Last name	Cake
1	Agatha	Endflick	cheesecake
2	Brenda	Flatter	gâteau
3	Christine	Griddle	angel food
4	Deborah	Henpeck	sponge

At Sleepyville's annual fair, the judges are about to announce the winner of the cake-making competition. Unfortunately, someone has written the results incorrectly, and although each item appears in the correct column, only one item in each column is correctly positioned. The following facts are true about the correct order:

1) The angel food cake is not second.
2) Brenda is two places before Flatter.
3) Either Endflick or Flatter is fourth.
4) Either Christine or Deborah finished just after a person (either Endflick or Flatter) who made either the angel food cake or sponge cake.
5) The gâteau finished either two places above or two places below the angel food cake.

Can you give the correct first name, last name, and cake for each position?

Solution on page 62.

Secret Message 1

The British have a secret agent somewhere in Germany. "The Shadow," as he is known, is ready to make his move. The Secret Service are waiting to receive communication from him about his location in order to make contact. The enigmatic message seen below arrives by mail. To decode it, remove one letter from each box so that no letter is repeated in any row or column.

FI	IU	IN	DR
BM	EM	BN	EY
AB	AE	AY	RY
EF	EU	NT	HU

Can you decode the message?

Solution on page 70.

Paying for Pizza

Five friends were ordering a pizza to share between them. Antwit had $1, Babble had $2, Crumble had $3, Dibdib had $4, and Earwig had $5. The cashier asked how they would be paying; in unison, they said, "We'll pay you with exact change!" The cashier then asked *which* of them would be paying, and each then claimed that some combination of two of them had exactly enough to cover the cost of the pizza.

Antwit said, "Me and Crumble or Dibdib."
Babble said, "Me and Dibdib or Earwig."
Crumble said, "Me and Babble or Dibdib."
Dibdib said, "Me and Antwit or Earwig."
Earwig said, "Me and Antwit or Babble."
Exactly three were lying. What was the cost of the pizza?

Solution on page 62.

Card Sharp 1

Shown above are three face-down cards and the queen of clubs. The following facts are true about the four cards:

1) No two suits are the same.
2) Exactly two face-down cards total 20.
3) No card to the left of the queen of clubs has a prime number value.
4) The heart and spade total 10.
5) The second card, which is a heart or diamond, makes a total of 21 with one other card.

An ace's value is 1, a jack's is 11, a queen's is 12, and a king's is 13. Can you identify the face-down cards?

Solution on page 59.

The Ticket Office

Three men (Andy, Bert, and Christopher) and three women (Doris, Ethel, and Felicity) are lined up to buy tickets to a rock concert by the Ungrateful Morons. The following facts are true about their order.

1) Christopher is in front of Andy.
2) Felicity is behind but not next to Ethel.
3) No two men are adjacent.
4) Felicity is next to neither Andy or Bert.

Can you determine their order in the line?

Solution on page 75.

Digital Deletions 3

$$8 \ 7 \ 6 \ 5$$
$$- \ 3 \ 7 \ 8 \ 9$$
$$\overline{4 \ 9 \ 7 \ 6}$$

In the subtraction problem above, delete one digit from each row (closing up the gaps in each case) to leave three columns of digits that still form a correct subtraction problem. Then repeat the process, erasing a second digit from each row to leave two columns, and finally a third to leave one column, closing the gaps to leave a correct subtraction after each deletion as before. Which numbers should be deleted and in what order?

Solution on page 70.

Secret Message 2

A foreign spy somewhere in California learned the CIA was aware of his presence and decided the safest plan would be to relocate and hide out in Utah for a while. An agent learned of his plan and sent the below message to headquarters. To decode it, remove one letter from each box so that no letter is repeated in any row or column.

FR	OR	NO	FM
AO	RX	NX	AB
MR	DR	OT	MO
MO	DO	AN	BO

Can you decode the message?

Solution on page 72.

The Greatest Composer

	First name	Last name	Masterpiece
1	George	Houndel	*Miss Iowa*
2	Foxgang	Moatsboat	*The Magic Fruit*
3	Loudhair	Fishoven	*Mood Lighting Sonata*
4	Ricky	Waggler	*Ride of the Valley Girl*

Musical Moments magazine has just published the results of its readers poll for the greatest classical composer (and their masterpieces). However, the pagesetter seems to have had a bad day; although each item is in the correct column, only one item in each column is correctly positioned. The following facts are true about the correct order.

1) Houndel is not second.
2) *Mood Lighting Sonata* is one place above Waggler.
3) Neither *The Magic Fruit* nor *Mood Lighting Sonata* are first.
4) George is one place above Houndel.
5) Neither George nor Loudhair are third.

Can you give the correct first name, last name, and masterpiece for each position?

Solution on page 76.

Card Sharp 2

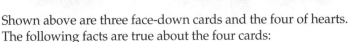

Shown above are three face-down cards and the four of hearts. The following facts are true about the four cards:

1) No two suits are the same.
2) The club, which is at one end of the row, totals 18 with the spade.
3) The fourth card has a lower value than 8.
4) Two adjacent cards have an identical value.
5) The club and the diamond total 12.

An ace's value is 1, a jack's is 11, a queen's is 12, and a king's is 13. Can you identify the face-down cards?

Solution on page 74.

A Fine Line

Four women, Alice, Barbara, Christine, and Denise, and two men, Edward and Frank, stand in a line.

1) Neither Barbara nor Denise stands next to another woman.
2) Edward is next to neither Alice nor Denise.
3) Denise is one, two, or three places to the right of Christine.

In what order do the six stand in the line, from left to right?

Solution on page 58.

Paper Trial

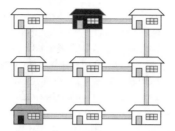

Rabbit, the newspaper delivery boy, sets off from the newsagent (indicated in gray) every morning to deliver newspapers to some of the seven houses in his neighborhood in Curious City. His route is finished when he arrives back at his home (indicated in black).

How many ways can Rabbit travel from the newsagent to his home without traversing the same gray path more than once? (He may pass the same house more than once as long as he uses different paths.)

Solution on page 76.

Digital Deletions 4

$$
\begin{array}{r}
3\ 8\ 6\ 7 \\
+\ 3\ 7\ 8\ 7 \\
\hline
7\ 6\ 5\ 4 \\
-\ 5\ 7\ 8\ 9 \\
\hline
1\ 8\ 6\ 5
\end{array}
$$

In the sequence of addition and subtraction problems above, delete one digit from each row (closing up the gaps in each case) to leave three columns of digits that still form a correct set of arithmetic problems. Then repeat the process, erasing a second digit from each row to leave two columns, and finally a third to leave one column, closing the gaps to leave correct addition and subtraction results after each deletion as before. Which numbers should be deleted and in what order?

Solution on page 73.

Crazy Cars

Eight local car owners are being questioned by Officer Nab about who bumped into the treasured 1969 Cadillac DeVille parked in his driveway. All he knows is that the offending vehicle was a Corvette, Mustang, or Tesla. Antwit has a Corvette, Earwig owns a Mustang, Dibdib drives a Tesla, Hogwash has a Corvette and a Mustang, Fritter drives a Corvette and a Tesla, Gripe has a Mustang and a Tesla, Babble owns all three, and Crumble's car is none of those three. Four of the owners who know who the culprit is make a statement about that person's identity.

Antwit says, "The driver has at least one car, but does not have a Corvette."

Babble says, "Either the driver doesn't own either a Mustang or Corvette, or the driver does not have a Tesla, but not both."

Crumble says, "Either the driver owns both a Corvette and Tesla, or the driver doesn't own either a Corvette or Tesla."

Dibdib says "The driver owns at least two cars, one of which is a Mustang."

Exactly one of the four statements is false. Which one of the eight drivers dented Officer Nab's Cadillac?

Solution on page 74.

Spinning Spades

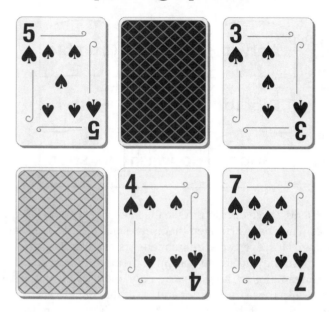

The latest teaser from the Card Conundrum Club consists of six spades arranged as shown. Club members are given the following information: The cards have been selected from three decks, which have black, gray, and white backs. There is at least one card from each deck in the array of six cards. The black-backed cards total 26. There are no face cards, and the ace has a value of 1.

The challenge is to test two propositions. First: "Every gray-backed card has a value that is at least 6." Second: "Exactly two black-backed cards have odd-numbered values." How many cards (and which ones) is it necessary to turn over to test each proposition?

Solution on page 63.

Moving Picture 1

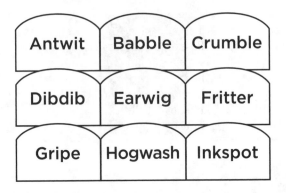

Nine friends have decided to see the latest *Rocky* sequel at the movies. They have arranged themselves in a 3×3 grid of seats as shown. However, an argument ensues over rights to the popcorn, so they decide to rearrange themselves. Consequently, only one remains in the same row, only one remains in the same column, and those two do not end up seated next to each other either vertically or horizontally. The following facts are true about their final arrangement:

1) Inkspot is in a column somewhere to the right of Gripe.
2) Earwig is somewhere in the row just below Inkspot.
3) Babble is in the same column as Gripe.
4) Crumble's row is two rows above Babble.
5) Hogwash is somewhere in the column immediately to the right of Dibdib.
6) Antwit is in a row somewhere above Dibdib.

Can you deduce their new arrangement?

Solution on pages 66–67.

Uneggspected

Mr. Bean the chocolate egg inspector is visiting the Falls Egg Factory. He finds four Easter baskets on display in a line, each with a different label. Basket A says it contains dark chocolate eggs; basket B advertises eggs filled with mint cream; basket C should contain eggs filled with strawberry jam; and the label of basket D indicates white chocolate eggs. Unfortunately, Mr. Bean discovers that no basket contains the correct kind of chocolate eggs. He makes some notes and leaves them on the baskets, so the factory workers can pass a follow-up inspection:

- On basket A, his note says, "The correct chocolates for this basket are in basket B."
- Basket B's note says, "The correct chocolates for this basket are in basket D."
- Basket C's note says, "The correct chocolates for this basket are in basket B or D."
- Basket D's note says, "The correct chocolates for this basket are in basket A or C."

Each basket contains exactly one kind of chocolate egg, and (because Mr. Bean did not wish to make it easy for the factory workers) he left a fifth note revealing that exactly two of the notes on the baskets are false, and that the eggs belonging in the baskets with false notes are not currently in adjacent baskets. Which notes are true, and where are all the eggs?

Solution on page 65.

Shifting Shapes

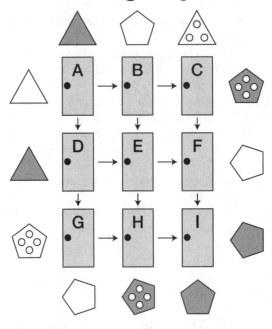

Seen above are the doors to nine workshops labeled A–I, surrounded by triangles and pentagons. Each shape on the left has passed through the three workshops directly to its right and has been transformed into the shape on the far right (e.g., the shape to the left of A has passed through workshops A, B, and C to finish as the one to the right of C). Similarly, each shape at the top has passed through the three workshops directly below it to finish as shown at the bottom. Each workshop always performs exactly one of these seven single operations (and performs that change on both shapes that enter it): drilling holes, filling in holes, rotating a shape 90° counterclockwise, painting the shape white, painting the shape gray, increasing the number of sides of a shape, or decreasing the number of sides of a shape. No more than one of the same change occurs in any row or column, and for any particular change there are at most two occurrences out of the nine. What does each workshop do?

Solution on page 94.

The Logical Library

It was Miss Take's first day as assistant at the Logical Library. However, it did not take long for her to notice an apparent irregularity. The seven books by the author Dee Stain had not been placed on the shelf in alphabetical order by their titles. So she rearranged them into what she thought was the correct order: *Awful Aunties, Boring Baking, Creepy Cottages, Desperate Dating, Eerie Espionage, Fractious Friends,* and *Ghoulish Games.*

When Mr. Prim saw what she had done, he was livid. He told her to put them back immediately, but she didn't remember anything about the original order. He then informed her that he would fire her if she failed to restore the proper order, which he described as follows:

1) No book title should be in its correct alphabetic position.
2) *Boring Baking* is either adjacent to *Ghoulish Games* or is three places from it.
3) *Awful Aunties* is two places from *Eerie Espionage*.
4) *Creepy Cottages* is three places from *Desperate Dating*.
5) *Fractious Friends* is four places from *Ghoulish Games*.

Mr. Prim then left for his lunch break, but not before haughtily announcing, "Unfortunately, that information will not be sufficient for you to uniquely determine the correct order. If I were to tell you whether *Awful Aunties* were to the left or right of *Desperate Dating*, you could manage it, but I don't think I will." What he didn't realize was that by saying that, he gave Miss Take enough information to definitively determine the original order. Can you do the same?

Solution on page 77.

The Crushed Cactus

The five siblings in the Drivel family (Egbert, Gravel, Jabber, Mudpot, and Spod) have been asked to stand in a line before their father. Someone has dropped an unabridged dictionary on his prize cactus and he intends to find out which one is responsible.

Jabber is at least three places from Gravel, and does not stand next to Egbert. From the children's perspective, Spod is somewhere to Mudpot's left, and Egbert is somewhere to Mudpot's right. Four of the children are asked about who had done the deed.

Egbert says "It was someone standing next to me."

Mudpot says, "It was someone at one end of the row."

Jabber says, "It was the person to my right."

Spod says, "It was the person standing two to my right."

Exactly two of the four are lying. Which one of the five Drivel children crushed the cactus?

Solution on page 73.

Digital Deletions 5

```
    7 1 9 6
  − 3 4 6 8
    ───────
    3 7 2 8
  + 4 5 6 9
    ───────
    8 2 9 7
```

In the sequence of subtraction and addition problems above, delete one digit from each row (closing up the gaps in each case) to leave three columns of digits that still form a correct set of arithmetic problems. Then repeat the process, erasing a second digit from each row to leave two columns, and finally a third to leave one column, closing the gaps to leave correct addition and subtraction results after each deletion as before. Which numbers should be deleted and in what order?

Solution on page 77.

The Solar Society 2

At the February meeting of the Solar Society, the five members who attend sit in a circle on five equally spaced chairs (numbered as shown above) facing the image of the Sun on the tiled floor. At the midpoint of the meeting, they decide to emulate orbiting planets by changing positions in the circle. The group leader for the month begins the meeting seated in chair 1. At no time does more than one person occupy a chair. Their movements as viewed from above the circle are as follows.

1) Mr. Mercury, who did not finish next to Mr. Uranus, moved to a chair two places clockwise.
2) Ms. Venus moved to a chair three places counterclockwise.
3) Mr. Jupiter, who is not February's group leader, exchanged position with Mr. Uranus; neither man was originally seated next to the person who finally occupied chair 1.
4) Ms. Saturn moved to a chair one place clockwise.

Can you deduce the initial and final seating arrangements?

Solution on page 68.

Screen Test

	First name	Last name	1st word of film title	2nd word of film title
1	Audrey	Hopeburn	*Romaine*	*Holiday*
2	Elizabeth	Dressmaker	*National*	*Velour*
3	Greta	Garbanzo	*Grand*	*Motel*
4	Meryl	Stripe	*Sofa*	*Choice*

Chris Critter, the film critic for *Movie Memories* magazine, has just published his list of the best actresses of all time, along with what he considers their greatest films. However, the list was transcribed incorrectly, and although the correct entries are in each column, only one item in each column is correctly positioned. The following facts are true about the correct order.

1) *National* is not next to *Grand*.
2) *Velour* is one place above Dressmaker.
3) Audrey is one place above *Choice*.
4) Dressmaker is not in the same position as *Grand*.
5) Elizabeth is one place below *National*.
6) Garbanzo is one place above *Grand*.

Can you find the actresses' full names and movie titles for each position?

Solution on page 80.

Lousy Electrics 2

An apartment has six rooms: a bathroom, bedroom, den, dining room, kitchen, and living room. In each room is a light switch and a light fixture, but the electrical wiring has been incorrectly installed. The light switches in exactly two of the six rooms control the light in the same room. For the other four rooms, each switch activates a light in a different room (there being only one switch connected to each light).

light fixtures

	bathroom	bedroom	den	dining room	kitchen	living room
bathroom						
bedroom						
den						
dining room						
kitchen						
living room						

switches

1) The living room switch activates the bedroom, dining room, or living room light.
2) The kitchen switch is not connected to the bedroom, dining room, or kitchen light.
3) The living room light is controlled by the bedroom, kitchen, or living room switch.
4) The bedroom light is not controlled by the switch in the bedroom, den, or dining room.
5) The bedroom switch activates the bathroom or living room light.
6) The bathroom light is not controlled by the bathroom, dining room, or kitchen switch.
7) The bathroom switch does not control the kitchen light.

Can you determine which switches control which lights?

Solution on page 78.

Professor Neuron's Age

Professor Neuron's nephew Trifle is interested in his uncle's age, so on one particular day of the week he asks Neuron's three sons; he asks them three times and each time he gets an oblique answer. On each occasion when he asks, only two sons are in the room, and one whispers information to the other who then reports to Trifle. Although two of them always tell the truth, the other one always lies, and Trifle has no idea who the liar is. A liar not only whispers the wrong information to the other person, but also takes whispered information and contradicts it. In contrast, a truth-teller whispers the correct information and faithfully reports whispered information whether correct or not. Each time that Trifle asks Professor Neuron's age, a different pair of Neuron's sons are in the room. The three answers that Trifle receives are as follows:

1) His age is not six times the number of letters in the name of this day of the week.
2) His age is not seven times the number of letters in the name of this day of the week.
3) His age is not a square number.

Trifle knows that his uncle's age is further from 40 than it is from 50. How old is Professor Neuron?

Solution on page 64.

Balance of Payment

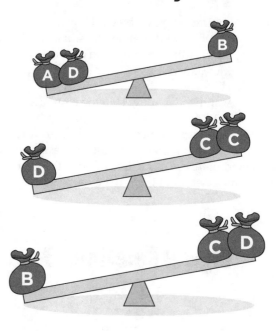

Mr. Colin Detts, a financial adviser who manages Toulouse Capital, keeps bags of gold coins in his safe. When business is quiet, he passes the time by weighing them against each other on the three balances in his office. There are five different types of bag (A, B, C, D, and E) with whole-number weights from 1 to 5 inclusive, although not necessarily in that order. Bags with the same letter all have identical weights, and no two bags with different letters weigh the same. One arrangement of the bags on the three balances is shown above. The scales tip to reveal that bags A and D combined are heavier than B, bag D alone is heavier than two of the bags marked C, and bag B alone is heavier than C and D together.

What are the weights of the five bags A–E?

Solution on page 63.

Gullible Garage

On Sunday Mr. Squidge stopped by Gullible Garage, which is run by the four members of the Kwakfit family, to ask which of the next six days his Cadillac will be ready for collection.

Aaron said, "Monday, Wednesday, or Friday."

Darren said, "Tuesday, Wednesday, or Saturday."

Karen said, "Monday, Tuesday, Thursday, or Saturday."

Sharon said, "Tuesday, Thursday, or Saturday."

However, Mr. Squidge has never trusted the four Kwakfits, as he knows that some family members always lie and some always tell the truth, and there are more liars than truth-letters. On what day can Mr. Squidge expect his car to be ready?

Solution on page 77.

Digital Deletions 6

$$
\begin{array}{r}
4\ 2\ 9\ 5 \\
+\ 4\ 3\ 7\ 8 \\
\hline
8\ 6\ 7\ 3 \\
-\ 4\ 7\ 4\ 8 \\
\hline
3\ 9\ 2\ 5
\end{array}
$$

In the sequence of addition and subtraction problems above, delete one digit from each row (closing up the gaps in each case) to leave three columns of digits that still form a correct set of arithmetic problems. Then repeat the process, erasing a second digit from each row to leave two columns, and finally a third to leave one column, closing the gaps to leave correct addition and subtraction results after each deletion as before. Which numbers should be deleted and in what order?

Solution on page 81.

Crime and Disorder

	Nickname	Last name	crime	state
1	Awful	Krane	burglary	Arizona
2	Brutish	Load	robbery	Florida
3	Crusher	Menace	mugging	Georgia
4	Dangerous	Nerd	fraud	Texas
5	Evil	Oval	vandalism	Wyoming

The most recent episode of the TV show *America's Not Necessarily Most Wanted, but Still Wanted* profiled five criminals on the run from the law, detailing what they were wanted for and in which state they were last seen. A chart at the end of the episode listed all five in order of the lengths of their crime sprees, but due to a transmission error, although each item in the chart is in the correct column, only one item in each column is correctly positioned. The following facts are true about the correct order.

1) Dangerous is two places below Florida.
2) Menace is two places above Awful and one above robbery.
3) Wyoming and Evil are in the same position.
4) Oval is three places below Georgia and one below fraud.
5) Vandalism is three places below Nerd.

Can you find the correct nickname and last name for each convict, their crime, and the state in which they were last seen?

Solution on page 71.

Moving Picture 2

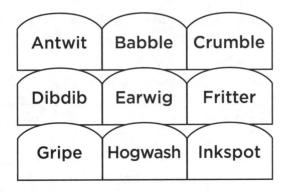

Antwit	Babble	Crumble
Dibdib	Earwig	Fritter
Gripe	Hogwash	Inkspot

Nine friends have decided to see the latest *Star Wars* sequel at the movies. They have arranged themselves in a 3×3 grid of seats as shown. However, an argument ensues after one of them refuses to remove his Darth Vader helmet, and they decide to rearrange themselves. Consequently, only one remains in the same row, and only one remains in the same column. The following facts are true about their final arrangement:

1) Antwit is in a row somewhere above Earwig.
2) Earwig is somewhere in the column immediately to the right of Dibdib.
3) Inkspot is in a column somewhere to the left of Antwit.
4) Crumble is in a column somewhere to the right of Dibdib.
5) Dibdib is in a row somewhere below Hogwash.
6) Hogwash is in a row somewhere below Babble.

Can you deduce their new arrangement?

Solution on page 82.

Movie Makeup

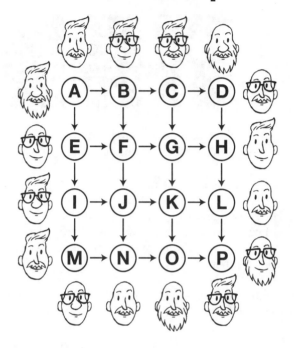

Stefan Spoolbag's latest movie is using so many extras that they need 16 makeup rooms. These are shown above, labeled A–P, surrounded by faces. Each face on the left has passed through the four rooms directly to the right and has been transformed into the face on the far right (e.g., the face to the left of A has passed through A, B, C, and D to finish as the one to the right of D). Similarly, each face at the top has passed through the four rooms directly below it to finish as shown at the bottom. Each room always performs one of these ten single alterations (and each must perform a change to both faces that enter it): adding or removing hair, adding or removing a beard, narrowing or widening a nose, adding or removing glasses, and adding or removing a mustache. No more than one of the same change occurs in any row or column.

What does each makeup room do?

Solution on page 69.

Card Sharp 3

Shown above are three face-down cards and the king of diamonds. The following facts are true about the four cards:

1) No two suits are the same.
2) The spade is not adjacent to a face card.
3) The second and third cards total 20.
4) Either the two red or the two black cards total 18.
5) Two face-down cards are face cards that are not adjacent to each other.

An ace's value is 1, a jack's is 11, a queen's is 12, and a king's is 13. Can you identify the face-down cards?

Solution on page 89.

False Filasteins

At the Filastein Faculty of Science, Dibdib and Earwig study physics only, Antwit and Gripe study chemistry only, Crumble and Fritter study both, and Babble and Hogwash study neither. Four of them are asked which of the eight has just been named dean.

Antwit says, "The dean is not one of the professors that studies only physics, nor one that studies only chemistry."

Babble says, "The dean studies neither physics nor chemistry."

Crumble says "The dean either studies only physics, or neither physics nor chemistry."

Dibdib says, "The dean's name has seven letters."

Exactly three are lying, and the dean is not a liar. Which of the eight has been named dean?

Solution on pages 78–79.

Digital Deletions 7

$$
\begin{array}{r}
4\ 7\ 3\ 8 \\
+\ 1\ 8\ 5\ 6 \\
\hline
6\ 5\ 9\ 4 \\
-\ 2\ 9\ 6\ 5 \\
\hline
3\ 6\ 2\ 9 \\
+\ 4\ 5\ 3\ 8 \\
\hline
8\ 1\ 6\ 7
\end{array}
$$

In the sequence of addition and subtraction problems above, delete one digit from each row (closing up the gaps in each case) to leave three columns of digits that still form a correct set of arithmetic problems. Then repeat the process, erasing a second digit from each row to leave two columns, and finally a third to leave one column, closing the gaps to leave correct addition and subtraction results after each deletion as before. Which numbers should be deleted and in what order?

Solution on page 83.

Cinema Sin

Antwit, Babble, Crumble, Dibdib, and Earwig are at the Hollywood Cinema to see the latest blockbuster. Only four of them have paid for a seat, though, the fifth having sneaked in behind the others. However, the manager, Mr. Saltcorn, has been alerted and asks each one of them to identify the interloper.

Antwit says, "Crumble or Dibdib."
Babble says, "Antwit or Earwig."
Crumble says, "Babble or Dibdib."
Dibdib says, "Babble or Crumble."
Earwig says, "Antwit, Crumble, or myself."

The manager has no idea how many are lying but has known their families for years and is sure that the person he is looking for is moral enough to tell the truth. Who snuck in without paying?

Solution on page 71.

Court Disaster

In the town of Little Gamble, the method of administering justice in a court of law leaves much to be desired. The judges evaluate the pleas of the accused by throwing a regular six-sided die twice. If the two numbers (1–6) are equal, the defendant is found guilty; if the values are different he is declared innocent.

In a recent case, the judge threw two numbers that totaled a prime number. For his private amusement, the court recorder wrote down five statements about the two numbers as follows.

1) The first number is odd.
2) At least one of the two numbers is square.
3) The second number is greater than 3.
4) The difference between the numbers is greater than 1.
5) The first is less than the second.

Unfortunately, the court recorder was also keeping track of a different court (checking his phone repeatedly for tennis tournament results), so his attention was lacking, and exactly one of his five statements was false. What are the two numbers that the judge threw on the dice?

Solution on page 67.

Lousy Electrics 3

An apartment has six rooms: a bathroom, bedroom, den, dining room, kitchen, and living room. In each room is a light switch and a light fixture, but the electrical wiring has been incorrectly installed. The light switch in only one of the six rooms controls the light in the same room. For the other five rooms, each switch activates a light in a different room (there being only one switch connected to each light).

light fixtures

	bathroom	bedroom	den	dining room	kitchen	living room
bathroom						
bedroom						
den						
dining room						
kitchen						
living room						

switches

1) Neither the bathroom nor the kitchen switch controls the light in the bedroom or dining room.
2) The bedroom switch does not activate the bathroom, bedroom, kitchen, or living room light.
3) The living room light is not controlled by the kitchen switch.
4) The living room switch does not control the light in the bathroom or bedroom.
5) The dining room light is not wired to the bedroom, dining room, or living room switch.

Can you determine which switches control which lights?

Solution on pages 80–81.

Lunches and Lies

In Alfonso's Italian Diner there are three pizza toppings on the menu: chicken, pepperoni, and anchovies. Antwit chose chicken only, Crumble had anchovies only, Earwig pepperoni only, Babble picked chicken and anchovies, Dibdib had anchovies and pepperoni, Fritter ate chicken and pepperoni, Gripe all three, and Hogwash none of them. Alfonso, the owner, wants to know who is paying the bill so four of the diners make a statement about the identity of that person.

Antwit says, "It's someone who did not have chicken, and did not have both anchovies and pepperoni."

Babble says "It's either someone who had both chicken and pepperoni, or someone who did not have either anchovies or pepperoni."

Crumble says "It's either someone who did not have either chicken or pepperoni, or someone who had both chicken and anchovies."

Dibdib says "It's someone who had chicken or anchovies (or both), and did not have pepperoni."

Exactly two are lying, and the bill payer does not utter a lie. Which one of the eight diners pays the bill?

Solution on page 79.

Phoney Statements

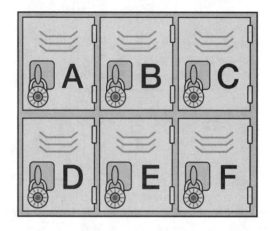

Six friends, Antwit, Babble, Crumble, Dibdib, Earwig, and Fritter, each had their own school locker labeled with their initials, as shown above. One of the six had stolen Trudge's cellphone and hidden it in their locker. All six friends knew which one of them had it. When questioned, each made a statement about the location of the missing phone.

1) Antwit said, "It's one column to the right of my locker."
2) Babble said, "It's in the same row as my locker."
3) Crumble said, "It's in a different row and column than my locker."
4) Dibdib said, "It's in the rightmost column."
5) Earwig said, "It's not in the row above mine."
6) Fritter said, "It's in a different column than my locker."

The trouble was, exactly two of them were lying. Who was lying, and who took the phone?

Solution on page 64.

Digital Deletions 8

```
    3 9 1 4
  + 1 2 4 9
  ─────────
    5 1 6 3
  - 3 4 1 5
  ─────────
    1 7 4 8
  + 2 6 1 4
  ─────────
    4 3 6 2
```

In the sequence of addition and subtraction problems above, delete one digit from each row (closing up the gaps in each case) to leave three columns of digits that still form a correct set of arithmetic problems. Then repeat the process, erasing a second digit from each row to leave two columns, and finally a third to leave one column, closing the gaps to leave correct addition and subtraction results after each deletion as before. Which numbers should be deleted and in what order?

Solution on page 87.

Cafeteria Caper

Five students are in front of the school principal accused of breaking in to the cafeteria storeroom. Apparently, Agatha, Benny, Catweed, Dribble, and Ethel climbed in through the window one after the other, though not necessarily in that order.

Agatha said, "Dribble was two places before Catweed."
Benny said, "I was one place either before or after Ethel."
Dribble said, "I was three places either before or after Agatha."
Ethel said, "Agatha was two places before me."

The principal knew that exactly one of them was lying because he already knew the order. He told the vice principal who the liar was, and she was able to definitively determine the students' order. In what order did the five of them climb through the storeroom window?

Solution on page 75.

Costume Competition

	First name	Last name	Town	Costume
1	Andrea	Bottle	Arcata	carrot
2	Cuthbert	Haggis	Jackson	robot
3	Edith	Mop	Pella	penguin
4	Gordon	Whinge	Tumwater	witch

The winners of the costume competition are about to be announced. However, the judges are wearing masks, which has made it difficult for them to see what they are writing. Although they have written each item in the correct column, only one item in each column is correctly positioned. The following facts are true about the correct order.

1) The person who came as a penguin is one place below the person from Pella but two places below Gordon.
2) Mop is two places above Edith.
3) Bottle is one place below the person who came as a robot but one place above the person from Tumwater.

Can you find each contestant's full name and hometown, and what costume each one wore?

Solution on page 84.

Carrot Confusion

Antwit, Babble, Crumble, Dibdib, and Earwig are visiting the open market. As they pass a greengrocer's stall, one of them decides to take a carrot and pocket it without paying. Mr. Root, the proprietor, has noticed the carrot's disappearance and asks each of the five to identify the prankster.

Antwit says, "Babble or Crumble."

Babble says, "Antwit, Dibdib, or Earwig."

Crumble says, "Antwit, Babble, or Earwig."

Dibdib says, "Antwit, Crumble, or me."

Earwig says, "The guilty one is lying."

Mr. Root is an expert at body language and can tell that at least three of them are lying. Which one of the five has the carrot?

Solution on page 60.

Counting Sheep

1	1	4	9	6	8	4	9
7	9	8	1	4	2	4	6
2	8	3	6	5	4	7	8
5	9	6	3	4	3	5	7
9	5	5	7	3	5	7	3
8	2	7	7	6	5	5	4
9	8	7	4	9	6	3	1
5	5	2	6	7	8	3	9

Above are 64 pens each containing a number of sheep. A buyer bought all the sheep in 16 of the pens: two pens from each row, and two pens from each column. After he took the sheep he had bought, each row and column contained exactly 30 sheep. Can you find the 16 pens from which he bought his sheep?

Solution on page 59.

Time to Retire

One of Officer Nab's tires has been stolen from the car in his driveway, and he's been informed that one of four friends took it as a prank. So he gets Antwit, Babble, Crumble, and Dibdib together and asks who took it. On each occasion when he asks, only two of the four are in the room and one whispers information to the other, who then reports it to him. Although two of them always tell the truth, the other two habitually lie, and Officer Nab has no idea who the liars are. A liar not only whispers the wrong information to the other person but also takes whispered information and contradicts it. In contrast, a truth-teller whispers the correct information and faithfully reports whispered information whether correct or not. On no two occasions when information is conveyed is Officer Nab in the room with the same combination of two people. The four answers that Officer Nab receives are as follows:

1) Crumble or Dibdib took it.
2) Antwit, Babble, or Dibdib took it.
3) Antwit, Crumble or Dibdib took it.
4) Antwit or Crumble took it.

Who stole Officer Nab's tire?

Solution on page 61.

Card Sharp 4

Shown above are three face-down cards, the jack of diamonds, and the five of spades. The following facts are true about the five cards.

1) There is at least one card of each suit, but no two cards of the same suit are adjacent.
2) Exactly two of the face-down cards total 20, and no more than one of those two cards is a heart.
3) There are two hearts, at least one of which is a face card.
4) The three rightmost cards total at most 13.

An ace's value is 1, a jack's is 11, a queen's is 12, and a king's is 13. Can you identify the face-down cards?

Solution on page 91.

Football Falsehoods

Eight friends are at the ticket window to get tickets for their home team's next three games, against the New York Jets, the Philadelphia Eagles, and the Chicago Bears. Dibdib will attend the Jets game, Babble the Eagles game, Hogwash the Bears game, Gripe both the Jets and Eagles games, Crumble the Eagles and Bears games, Antwit the Jets and Bears games, Fritter all three, and Earwig none of them. At the ticket office, the counter assistant asks who is paying for the tickets. Four of the friends make a statement about the identity of that person.

Crumble says "It's someone who's not attending the Jets game, and isn't attending both the Eagles and Bears games."

Earwig says, "It's someone who's attending the Eagles game, or someone who isn't attending either of the Jets or Bears games (or someone who fits both descriptions)."

Fritter says "It's either someone who isn't attending either of the Jets or Bears games, or someone who isn't attending either of the Eagles or Bears games (or someone who fits both descriptions)."

Gripe says "It's someone who's not attending either of the Jets or Eagles games, or someone who's attending the Bears game (or someone who fits both descriptions)."

Exactly two are lying, and the payer is not a liar. Which one of the eight football fans pays for the tickets?

Solution on page 92.

Digital Deletions 9

```
    8 3 4 6
  - 5 6 2 8
  ─────────
    2 7 1 8
  + 4 5 1 3
  ─────────
    7 2 3 1
  - 5 6 1 4
  ─────────
    1 6 1 7
```

In the sequence of addition and subtraction problems above, delete one digit from each row (closing up the gaps in each case) to leave three columns of digits that still form a correct set of arithmetic problems. Then repeat the process, erasing a second digit from each row to leave two columns, and finally a third to leave one column, closing the gaps to leave correct addition and subtraction results after each deletion as before. Which numbers should be deleted and in what order?

Solution on page 93.

Digital Deletions 10

```
    1 2 4 9
  + 4 9 3 6
  ─────────
    6 1 8 5
  - 2 3 5 8
  ─────────
    3 8 2 7
  + 4 9 1 9
  ─────────
    8 7 4 6
```

(See instructions for Digital Deletions 9 above.) Which numbers should be deleted and in what order?

Solution on page 96.

Lies and Legerdemain

 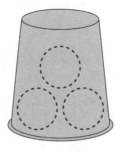 

Professor Neuron was performing his version of the famous cups and balls trick for his nephews. Three inverted cups—white, gray, and black—each have three balls underneath. Neuron takes a ball from under the white cup and secretly relocates it under either the gray or the black one. Then he takes one from under the gray cup and hides it under either the white or black one. Finally, he removes a ball from under the black cup and conceals it either under the white one, the gray one, or back under the black one. Neuron now makes three statements about the numbers of balls under the three cups as follows.

1) The total number of balls under the gray and black cups is smaller than 6.
2) The gray cup has more than 3 balls under it.
3) The total number of balls under the white and black cups is greater than 6.

Exactly one of his three statements is false. What are the number of balls under the three cups at the end of the trick?

Solution on page 83.

The Solar Society 3

At the March meeting of the Solar Society, the six members (including Mr. Saturn) who attend sit in a circle on six equally spaced chairs (numbered as shown above) facing the image of the Sun on the tiled floor. At the midpoint of the meeting, they decide to emulate orbiting planets by changing positions in the circle. The group leader for the month begins the meeting seated in chair 1. At no time does more than one person occupy a chair. Their positions and movements as viewed from above the circle are as follows.

1) Ms. Neptune moved one chair clockwise.
2) Ms. Venus did not start next to chair 1.
3) Mr. Jupiter, who does not finish next to Ms. Neptune, moved to the opposite seat.
4) Mr. Mercury and Ms. Venus, who are two places from each other, exchanged positions.
5) Mr. Uranus, who sits two places from chair 1, did not move.

Can you deduce the initial and final seating arrangements?

Solution on pages 84–85.

Coolio's Conundrum

Eight friends are visiting Coolio's Ice Cream Cavern. Fritter chooses chocolate ice cream, Crumble has strawberry, Hogwash orders vanilla, Dibdib has chocolate and strawberry, Gripe picks strawberry and vanilla, Antwit takes chocolate and vanilla, Earwig has all three flavors already mentioned, and Babble has butter pecan. As a prank, one of the eight friends switches off the refrigerator and all Coolio's ice cream melts. Losing his cool, Coolio confronts four of the eight friends at their table and demands that they identify the culprit. So each makes a statement.

Antwit says, "It was either someone who ate both chocolate and strawberry, or someone who didn't eat either strawberry or vanilla."

Dibdib says, "It was either someone who didn't eat either strawberry or vanilla, or someone who ate vanilla but not chocolate."

Fritter says, "It was either someone who ate both chocolate and vanilla, or someone who didn't eat either chocolate or vanilla."

Gripe says, "It was someone who didn't eat either strawberry or vanilla, or someone who ate chocolate (or someone who fits both descriptions)."

Of the four, two habitually told the truth, one habitually lied, while the other sometimes told the truth and sometimes lied. The culprit does not tell lies.

Which one of the eight friends turned off Coolio's refrigerator?

Solution on page 60.

Disordered Dogs

	First name	Last name	Age (in years)	Color
1	Chewbee	Doo	3	blue
2	Droolius	Caesar	6	green
3	Mary	Puppins	4	orange
4	Poodle	Wipes	8	red
5	Sherlock	Bones	7	white
6	Woofgang	Amadaypuss	5	yellow

All is not well at the greyhound races. Mr. Scribe, the race recorder, is suffering from memory loss and cannot recall the finishing order of the last race. Although each item is in the correct column, he only has one item in each column correctly positioned. Each dog has a first and last name, and the following facts are true about the correct order.

1) The 8-year-old dog is one place from Wipes.
2) The dog wearing orange is somewhere above Poodle, who is somewhere above Caesar.
3) Puppins is one place below Mary, who is two places below the 4-year-old.
4) The 3-year-old is three places above Sherlock, who is two below the dog wearing red.
5) Chewbee is one place below the 5-year-old, who is one below the dog wearing yellow.
6) The dog wearing blue is two places above Amadaypuss.

Can you give the dogs' correct full names, together with their ages and the colors they are wearing, for each position?

Solution on pages 86–87.

The School of Logic

Five candidates (Armature, Brush, Charge, Diode, and Electron) have applied for the position of electrical maintenance engineer in the School of Logic at Perspica City University, and each wants the job very badly. Before they attend, each receives a letter instructing them to adopt the role of truth-teller or liar at the interview but not to divulge their choice to anyone. All five are master logicians and excellent engineers, but one of them is the best candidate for the post, and they all agree as to who that is. Each is asked a single question at the interview, for which they are all present.

Armature is asked "Is exactly one of the following statements true: 'You are a liar' and 'The best candidate for the post is Armature or Diode'?"

Brush is asked "Is it correct to say that the following statements are either both true or both false: 'You are a truth-teller' and 'The best candidate for the post is Armature or Charge'?"

Charge is asked "Is exactly one of the following statements false: 'You are a truth-teller' and 'The best candidate for the post is Brush, Diode, or Electron'?"

Diode is asked "Is exactly one of the following statements true: 'You are a liar' and 'The best candidate for the post is Armature, Charge, or Electron'?"

Electron is asked "Are you happy right now?"

Exactly two of the five answered "no," which was enough to determine the best candidate.

Who is the best candidate for the post, and did Electron tell the truth or lie?

Solution on page 95.

Lousy Electrics 4

An apartment has seven rooms: a bathroom, bedroom, den, dining room, kitchen, library, and living room. In each room is a light switch and a light fixture, but the electrical wiring has been incorrectly installed. The light switches in exactly two of the seven rooms control the light in the same room. For the other five rooms, each switch activates a light in a different room (there being only one switch connected to each light).

light fixtures

	bathroom	bedroom	den	dining room	kitchen	library	living room
bathroom							
bedroom							
den							
dining room							
kitchen							
library							
living room							

switches

1) The bathroom light is not connected to the dining room or living room switch.
2) Neither the library nor the living room light is controlled by the switch in the bedroom, dining room, or kitchen.
3) The den switch doesn't affect the den or library light.
4) The living room light has no connection to the den or library switch.
5) The light in the kitchen is not wired to the bathroom or dining room switch.
6) Neither the bedroom nor the den switch operates the bathroom, bedroom, or kitchen light.

Can you determine which switches control which lights?

Solution on pages 88–89.

The Solar Society 4

At the April meeting of the Solar Society, the eight members who attend (including Ms. Saturn) sit in a circle on eight equally spaced chairs (numbered as shown above) facing the image of the Sun on the tiled floor. At the midpoint of the meeting, they decide to emulate orbiting planets by changing positions in the circle. The group leader for the month begins the meeting seated in chair 1. At no time does more than one person occupy a chair. Their positions and movements as viewed from above the circle are as follows.

1) Ms. Earth and Mr. Pluto, who sit two places apart, exchange positions.
2) Mr. Mercury moves three places counterclockwise.
3) Ms. Neptune moves to the opposite seat.
4) Ms. Venus, who starts next to neither Mr. Jupiter nor Mr. Uranus, moves one place clockwise.
5) Mr. Uranus and Mr. Jupiter, who sit three places apart, exchange places.
6) Mr. Pluto finishes opposite chair 1, closer to Mr. Uranus than to Mr. Jupiter, neither of whom is the group leader.

Can you deduce the initial and final seating arrangements?

Solution on pages 90–91.

Pentomime

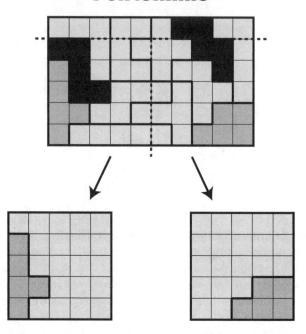

At the Battle of Bosworth Field in 1485, Henry Tudor was sitting in his tent admiring his set of 12 pentominoes. (A pentomino is an arrangement of five identical squares joined edge to edge; there are 12 possible such shapes.) Henry had arranged for his court mathematician to fit them all together on a 6×10 marble base. Suddenly, a lead cannonball whistled through the tent, shattering the marble base into three pieces, as indicated by the dotted lines. In the process, two of the pentominoes (shown in black) were destroyed but the other ten managed to survive intact. Two of the remaining three fragments of the marble base that remained were 5×5 squares, and one pentomino in each section (shown in dark gray) was still in position from the original arrangement.

How can the remaining eight pentominoes be fitted into the two squares? (Pentominoes may be rotated or flipped.)

Solution on page 87.

The Mind-Stretcher

A prisoner in solitary confinement, who has no idea what day of the week it is, has been told that on each day for three consecutive days he can ask the guard on duty a question to which he will receive a "yes" or "no" answer. From the responses, he must announce on the third day what day of the week it is. If he is correct he will be set free; if not he will be executed.

The prisoner is faced with several difficulties. Each guard will either consistently tell the truth or consistently lie, and there will be a different guard every day. Furthermore, although the guards understand English, they have been instructed only to answer "ho" or "mo," one of them meaning "yes" and the other meaning "no." The prisoner, however, has no idea which is which.

What line of questioning is sure to win the prisoner his freedom?

Solution on pages 92–93.

Answers

18 A Fine Line

Barbara, Edward, Christine, Alice, Frank, Denise.

Since neither Barbara nor Denise are standing next to another woman (per clue 1), and there are only two men, their positions must be one of the following (or their reflections): BM??MD, ??MBMD, or ??MDMB. The last one of those isn't possible, because both men are standing next to Denise, but per clue 2, Edward is not next to Denise. That leaves us with two options (and their reflections): BE??FD and ??EBFD. Since Edward is not next to Alice, either (also per clue 2), we can fill in the other two positions in both, giving us BECAFD and ACEBFD. Clue 3 tells us that Denise is to the right of Christine, so both those orientations are correct (and their reflections are not); however, in the second one, Denise is four places to the right of Christine, contradicting clue 3, leaving BECAFD as the only option.

44 Counting Sheep

1	1	4	9	6			9
	9	8	1	4	2		6
2	8	3	6		4	7	
5		6	3	4		5	7
	5		7	3	5	7	3
8	2			6	5	5	4
9		7	4		6	3	1
5	5	2		7	8	3	

15 Card Sharp 1

From clue 4, neither the heart nor spade can be greater than 9. From clue 2, one of these must total 20 with the third face-down card. The values that can total twenty (in which one card is less than 10) are 9 and 11, 8 and 12, or 7 and 13. Combining that with clue 4, the three face-down cards (in no particular order) can have the values 1, 9, and 11; 2, 8, and 12; or 3, 7, and 13. Let's consider clue 5. Since no two cards in any of these three triplets total 21, the queen of clubs (with a value of 12) must total 21 with a 9, and that 9 (per clue 5) is the second card and is a heart or diamond. Since the 9 is one of the cards that total 10 in clue 4, and those cards include a heart and spade, the 9 is a heart and the other card totaling 10 is the ace of spades. The fourth card is a diamond (per clue 1) with a value of 11 (that is, a jack). According to clue 3, the jack can't be to the left of the queen (since its value is 11, which is prime), so it's the fourth card, and the ace of spades is first.

7 Digital Deletions 1

```
  4 6 8        4 8        4
+ 3 2 8      + 2 8      + 2
  -----        ---        ---
  7 9 6        7 6        6
```

51 Coolio's Conundrum

Earwig turned off the refrigerator. The following table shows who each statement refers to, depending on whether those statements are true or false.

	True	False
A	BDEF	ACGH
D	BFGH	ACDE
F	ABCE	DFGH
G	ABDEF	CGH

Of the four speakers, there are either one or two liars. The only suspects to appear in exactly one or two false statements are Antwit, Dibdib, Earwig, and Fritter. However, if Antwit, Dibdib, or Fritter are responsible, they must be lying, and the culprit didn't lie, so Earwig (who makes no statement at all) is the guilty one.

44 Carrot Confusion

Dibdib took the carrot. Of the first four to speak, consider the number who are lying for each possible culprit. If it was Antwit, then only Antwit is lying. If it was Babble, then Babble and Dibdib are lying. If it was Crumble, then Babble and Crumble are lying. If it was Dibdib, then Antwit and Crumble are lying. If it was Earwig, then Antwit and Dibdib are lying. Therefore, no matter who took the carrot, the first four statements can contain at most two lies, and the third lie must be Earwig's statement. Since Earwig's statement is a lie, the culprit told the truth (which means Earwig is innocent). Dibdib is the only one who made a self-incriminating statement, and therefore is the guilty one.

8 The Solar Society 1

Mr. Jupiter is in chair 1, Mr. Mercury is in chair 2, Ms. Saturn is in chair 3, Mr. Uranus is in chair 4, Ms. Venus is in chair 5, and Ms. Neptune is in chair 6. Per clue 2, Mercury sits immediately to Saturn's right, and per clue 3, Venus sits two chairs to Jupiter's right. These two parts of the seating arrangement can't overlap, so there are two options (ignoring the question of which specific chairs they are in), from left to right: SMJ?V? or SM?J?V. One of those question marks must represent Uranus, which means the second option is impossible; in it, both empty chairs are next to Jupiter, but per clue 1, Jupiter is not seated next to Uranus. Therefore the first option is correct, and since Jupiter is not seated next to Uranus, the order is SMJNVU (going counterclockwise in some orientation). From clue 4, we know Uranus is seated in chair 3, 4, or 5. In chair 3, Mercury would be in chair 1 (contradicting clue 2, which states Mercury isn't the group leader); in chair 5, Saturn would be in chair 4, opposite the group leader (also contradicting clue 2). Uranus, therefore, is in chair 4, which fixes the final orientation.

45 Time to Retire

Babble took the tire.

With two truth-tellers and two liars (T_1, T_2, F_1, F_2), the possible pairs are T_1T_2, T_1F_1, T_1F_2, T_2F_1, T_2F_2, and F_1F_2. The only pairs that will deliver a true response are T_1T_2 and F_1F_2, so at most two of the four reported answers can be true. This means that anyone whose name appears more than twice among the answers cannot be the guilty one. Everyone's name appears three times except for Babble, who is mentioned only once, so the culprit must be Babble.

13 Cake Mix

	First name	Last name	Cake
1	Christine	Henpeck	gâteau
2	Brenda	Endflick	sponge
3	Deborah	Griddle	angel food
4	Agatha	Flatter	cheesecake

Per clue 2, Brenda and Flatter are, respectively, in positions 1 and 3 or positions 2 and 4. If Endflick were in position 4, then Flatter would have to be in position 3, but then it would be impossible for any name in that column to be in the correct position. Endflick therefore isn't in position 4, so Flatter is (per clue 3) and Brenda is correctly positioned in 2. No one finished after Flatter, so Endflick must be the person referenced in clue 4. Endflick can't be in 3 (since, again, it would then be impossible for any last name to be correctly positioned), so Endflick is in 2. The angel food cake isn't in 2 (per clue 1), so Endflick made the sponge cake. Christine can't be the person who finished after Endflick (since Brenda is already correctly positioned in that column), so it's Deborah. Per clue 5, the gâteau and angel food cake must be in positions 1 and 3 in some order. If the angel food is in 1, then it's impossible for any cake to be correctly positoned, so the angel food is in 3 and the gâteau in 1. No last name is correctly positioned yet; the only possibility is Griddle in 3. Bearing in mind that no remaining items are correctly placed, everything else can be placed by elimination.

14 Paying for Pizza

The pizza cost $6. If there are three liars there must be exactly two truth-tellers. The ten pairs mentioned in the statements (in order) are AC, AD, BD, BE, BC, CD, AD, DE, AE, and BE. Sorting those into pairs that have the same sum, we have pairs totaling $4 (AC), $5 (AD, BC, AD again), $6 (BD, AE), $7 (BE, CD, BE again), and $9 (DE). Since exactly two people told the truth, the correct amount must be the one that appears in exactly two statements, which is $6 (and the truth-tellers are Babble and Earwig).

11 Digital Deletions 2

```
  8 9 7        8 7          7
- 3 2 8      - 2 8        - 2
  -----        ----         ---
  5 6 9        5 9          5
```

21 Spinning Spades

For the first proposition, only the gray-backed card need be turned over. Since there is at least one white-backed card, either one, two, or three out of the four face-up cards, plus the face-down card with the black back, total 26. The maximum value the face-down black card can have is 10. The highest sum of two face-up cards is 12, so the cards adding up to 26 must include three face-up cards and must have black backs. The fourth face-up card has a white back, so the card with a gray back showing is the only gray-backed card, and all that's needed to test the proposition is to flip it over and see if its value is 6 or higher.

For the second proposition, no cards need be turned over. All of the above deductions still apply. The highest possible sum of three face-up cards is 16 $(4+5+7)$; to add up to 26 with those cards, the face-down card would have to be a 10. There are no cards higher than 10, so the face-up cards contributing to the sum of 26 cannot be smaller than 16, so the 4, 5, and 7 have black backs, and the face-down card is a 10 (and the 3 has a white back). We have now proven the proposition that exactly two black-backed cards are odd (the 5 and 7) without turning any cards over.

31 Balance of Payment

Bags A, B, C, D, and E weigh 4, 5, 1, 3, and 2 respectively.

$D>2C$ and C is at least 1, so D is at least 3, and $B>C+D$, so $C+D$ must be less than 5. Since the minimum values of C and D add up to 4, we can determine the values of B, C, and D: $B=5$, $C=1$, and $D=3$. From the top balance, $A+3>5$, so A must be 4, and E is 2 by elimination.

9 Pieces of Eight

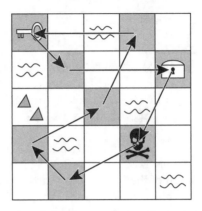

30 Professor Neuron's Age

Professor Neuron is 49. Since one of the three sons is a liar, only one of the three statements is true (the one which was reported to him by the pair of truth-telling sons). Statements 1 and 2 cannot both be false (since the statements were given on the same day), so one of them is true, which means Professor Neuron's is either six or seven times the number of letters in some day of the week. The lengths of the days of the week range from six to nine letters, so Professor Neuron's possible ages are 36, 42, 48, 49, 54, 56, and 63. Statement 3 must be false (since two statements are false), so Professor Neuron's age is a square number. Of the possible ages above, 36 and 49 are both square numbers, but 36 is further from 50 than it is from 40, so 49 is the correct age (and the statements were made on a Tuesday).

41 Phoney Statements

Babble and Dibdib were lying, and Earwig took the phone.

Statements 2 and 5 contradict each other, so one must be true and the other false. Likewise, statements 4 and 6 contradict each other, so the other false statement must be one of those. That means statements 1 and 3 are both true, and locker E is the only one described by both. Statements 5 and 6 also point to locker E, so statements 2 and 4 (from Babble and Dibdib) are the two lies.

23 Uneggspected

The statements on baskets C and D are true, and the eggs are currently ordered BCDA (with the letters referring to the baskets they should be in).

It is given that no basket contains its own eggs. The diagram below shows which basket each basket's eggs could be in, depending on whether that basket's note is true or false.

	True	False
A	B	CD
B	D	AC
C	BD	A
D	AC	B

Consider the notes on baskets C and D. If they are both false, then the notes on baskets A and B are both true. That's obviously impossible, because then two kinds of egg would be in basket B, with none in basket C. So at least one of the notes on baskets C and D must be true. Now, considering the same baskets, let's assume one note is true and one is false. If C is true and D is false, then between them they occupy B and D and it's impossible for the note on either basket A or B to be true. If C is false and D is true, then between them they occupy baskets A and C, which would mean the note on basket B must be true (if it's false, its eggs are in basket A or C, but both are occupied). So its eggs would be in basket D, and that would account for the second truthful note, so basket A's note would be false. But then its eggs would have to be in basket C or D, which is impossible. So once again we have a contradiction, and the notes on baskets C and D must both be true, with the other two notes being false.

The eggs from baskets B and D occupy baskets A and C in some order. That means A's eggs must be in basket D and C's eggs are in basket B. The eggs from the two baskets with false notes are not in adjacent baskets, so B's eggs aren't in basket C (where they'd be adjacent to A's) and are instead in basket A, with D's eggs in basket C.

22 Moving Picture 1

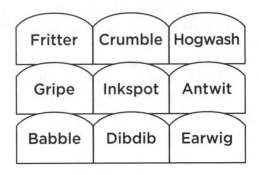

For convenience, let the statement "only one remains in the same row, only one remains in the same column, and those two do not end up seated next to each other either vertically or horizontally" be denoted by "X." From clue 4, Crumble is in the top row and must be the "same row" person in X, and Babble is in the bottom row. Per clue 2, Earwig is one row below Inkspot. Earwig cannot be in the middle row (which would violate X, as the "same row" person is accounted for), so Earwig is in the bottom row and Inkspot in the middle row. Antwit is not in the top (which would violate X), so from clue 6, Antwit is in the middle row and Dibdib in the bottom row. To avoid violating X, Fritter can't be in the middle row, but the bottom row is now full, so Fritter is in the top row. We can't yet determine which row Gripe and Hogwash are in, so let's look at the columns.

From clue 1, Gripe is in the left or middle column and Inkspot is in the middle or right column; they can't both be in the middle column, so at least one is in an edge column. But whichever one is in an edge column would be the "same column" person in X, so one of them is that person and the other is in the middle column. Per clue 3, Babble is in the same column as Gripe, but Babble would violate X by being in the middle column, so Babble and Gripe are in the left column (with Gripe staying in the same column), and Inkspot is in the middle column. Hogwash doesn't stay in the middle column (would violate X), so per clue 5, Hogwash is in the right column with Dibdib in the center column. Since we know both the row and column of Babble, Dibdib, and Inkspot, we can place them in their seats.

Since we've placed everyone else in the bottom row, Earwig must be in the rightmost seat in that row. In the middle row,

Antwit must change columns to avoid violating X, so Antwit sits in the rightmost seat of that row. This leaves only the uppermost seat of the right column for Hogwash. Since Crumble and Fritter have the remaining two positions left in the top row, Gripe must be in the leftmost seat in the middle row. Since Crumble and Gripe can't be in adjacent seats per X, Fritter sits in the leftmost seat of the top row and Crumble takes the middle seat.

38 Court Disaster

The first number is 3 and the second is 4.

The prime number total is 2, 3, 5, 7, or 11. For 2, we can only have 1/1, for which both (3) and (4) are false. For both options totaling 3 (1/2 and 2/1), both (3) and (4) are false. For 11, the rolls can be 5/6 or 6/5, but then both (2) and (4) are false. Of the possibilities that add up to 5, 1/4 satisfies all conditions, 2/3 and 3/2 contradict both (2) and (3), and 4/1 contradicts both (1) and (5). So the dice total 7, with the possible pairs of 1/6, 2/5, 3/4, 4/3, 5/2, and 6/1. The last three contradict both (3) and (5); 2/5 contradicts both (1) and (2); and 1/6 satisfies all conditions. Only 3/4 gives exactly one false statement.

10 Clues and Queues

Antwit, Babble, Earwig, Crumble, Fritter, Dibdib. (We'll refer to the six by their initials for convenience.) Combining clues 3 and 4 gives us 4 possible arrangments of D, E, and F in line: (i) D??E?F, (ii) E?FD??, (iii) ?E?FD?, or (iv) ??E?FD. Arrangement (i) is impossible, as no one could be in position 2; per clue 1, A is not next to D, and per clue 2, B and C would have to be in positions 3 and 5 in some order. No pair of unassigned positions in (ii) are two spaces apart, which contradicts clue 2, so we can eliminate that option as well. As for arrangement (iii), the situation is similar to arrangement (i) except position 6 is the one where no one could be (A is not next to D, and B and C would have to be in positions 1 and 3 in some order). So (iv) is correct. To fulfill clue 2, B and C must be in positions 2 and 4 in some order, so A is in position 1. Per clue 1, C is not next to A, so B is 2nd and C is 4th.

initial arrangement   **final arrangement**

The initial arrangement was: Mr. Uranus in chair 1, Ms. Saturn in chair 2, Ms. Venus in chair 3, Mr. Jupiter in chair 4, and Mr. Mercury in chair 5. After they moved, the arrangement was: Mr. Jupiter in chair 1, Mr. Mercury in chair 2, Ms. Saturn in chair 3, Mr. Uranus in chair 4, and Ms. Venus in chair 5.

Per clue 3, Jupiter and Uranus exchanged places, so no one else occupied either of their seats at any time. Saturn moved one chair clockwise (clue 4), so neither her starting or ending chair is one that Jupiter or Uranus sat in. That means her starting chair must have ended up with Mercury or Venus sitting in it, and her ending chair must be where either Mercury or Venus started. Per clues 1 and 2, Mercury and Venus both moved two chairs clockwise (moving three places counterclockwise is equivalent to moving two places clockwise), so we can also determine where their other seats must have been, and Jupiter and Uranus occupied the other two seats in some order. Let's refer to Mercury and Venus as A and B and Jupiter and Uranus as X and Y for now (we'll determine which is which later). The original seating arrangement must have been SAXBY (in some orientation) with the final arrangement being BSYAX. Per clue 1, Mercury did not finish next to Uranus, and A is next to both X and Y (one of whom must be Uranus), so A cannot be Mercury and therefore A is Venus and B is Mercury. Our updated arrangements are now SVXMY and MSYVX. In the second arrangement, Mercury is next to X (they are sitting in a circle), so X cannot be Uranus and therefore X is Jupiter and Y is Uranus. The two arrangements, then, are SVJMU and MSUVJ, and now we just need to determine the correct orientation. Per clue 3, neither Jupiter nor Uranus was seated next to the person who ended up in chair 1. One or both were adjacent to Venus, Mercury, and Saturn, so one of the two of them must have ended up seated in chair 1. Since they swapped places, whichever one of the two didn't end up in chair 1 must have started there. But Jupiter did not start in chair 1 (since he wasn't group leader, per clue 3), so he ended up there, and Uranus was group leader, which fixes the final orientation.

6 Psychic Sid

It will snow on Saturday. Since only one prediction is accurate, the correct day is the one that appears only once among all the predictions.

10 The Four Chairs

Babble	Crumble
Dibdib	Antwit

From clue 1, Babble is still in the top row, so must move to the upper left. Crumble must also change seats, and therefore moves to the right column. Per clue 2, then, Dibdib is in the left column (in the seat below Babble), which leaves the lower right seat for Antwit (per clue 1), and Crumble sits top right.

35 Movie Makeup

A: adding glasses; B: narrowing nose; C: removing hair; D: removing beard; E: widening nose; F: removing glasses; G: narrowing nose; H: adding hair; I: removing hair; J: adding mustache; K: removing glasses; L: narrowing nose; M: removing mustache; N: removing hair; O: adding beard; P: adding glasses.

16 Digital Deletions 3

```
  8 7 5        8 7          7
- 3 7 8      - 3 8        - 3
-------      -----        ---
  4 9 7        4 9          4
```

7 Salt and Pepper

Antwit has the salt, Babble has the pepper, and Crumble has neither. Since Antwit is lying, Crumble does not have the salt. And since Babble is lying, Crumble doesn't have the pepper either. Crumble, then, is effectively stating that Babble has the salt and Antwit has the pepper, but since the statement is a lie, it's the other way around.

14 Secret Message 1

The message is FIND ME BY BAYREUTH, indicating that the spy is located near the southern German city of Bayreuth.

	a	b	c	d
1	FI	IU	IN	DR
2	BM	EM	BN	EY
3	AB	AE	AY	RY
4	EF	EU	NT	HU

We'll label the rows and columns for convenience. Note that the set of squares (2a, 2b, 3a, 3b) contains four letters twice each, and has two possible orientations: (B, M, A, E) and (M, E, B, A). Another set of four squares with the same trait is (1a, 1b, 4a, 4b), which must be either (F, I, E, U) or (I, U, F, E). However, since we have already seen that either 2b or 3b contains an E, 4b cannot contain an E, so (F, I, E, U) is correct. With this information we can complete the grid by elimination.

33 Crime and Disorder

	Nickname	Last name	crime	state
1	Brutish	Load	mugging	Georgia
2	Crusher	Nerd	burglary	Florida
3	Evil	Menace	fraud	Wyoming
4	Dangerous	Oval	robbery	Arizona
5	Awful	Krane	vandalism	Texas

Per clue 4, fraud in is position 3 or 4, and per clue 5, vandalism is in position 4 or 5. If fraud were correctly placed in 4, vandalism would be forced to also be correctly placed in 5, which is impossible, so fraud is in 3 (and per clue 4, Georgia is in 1 and Oval is in 4). Now let's consider clue 2. Menace, robbery, and Awful are either in positions 1, 2, and 3 respectively, or positions 3, 4, and 5. (They aren't in 2, 3, and 4, because fraud is already in 3, so robbery can't be there.) Per clue 5, Nerd is three places above vandalism. If Nerd were in 1 and vandalism were in 4, that would conflict with both possible positions for the items in clue 2. Nerd being in 1 would block Menace in 1 (contradicting the first option) and vandalism being in 4 would block robbery in 4 (contradicting the second option). Nerd and vandalism, therefore, must be in positions 2 and 5 respectively (with vandalism correctly placed in 5). Since vandalism is correctly placed, robbery can't also be correctly placed in 2, so it must be in 4 (with Menace correctly placed in 3 and Awful in 5). There's now only one way to place the items in clue 1: Florida in 2 and Dangerous in 4, both correctly placed. That in turn leaves only one place for the items in clue 3: Wyoming and Evil are both in position 3. Given that nothing else can be correctly positioned, everything else can be placed by elimination.

37 Cinema Sin

Earwig was the one who entered without paying. If the culprit tells the truth, then they must include themselves in their statement. Earwig is the only one to have done so and therefore must be the guilty one.

11 Lousy Electrics 1

The bedroom switch controls the kitchen light; the dining room switch controls the bedroom light; the kitchen switch controls the dining room light; and the bathroom switch controls the bathroom light.

Per clue 1, the kitchen light isn't controlled by the switch in the kitchen or bathroom, and since the kitchen is downstairs, it's not controlled by the dining room switch either, per clue 2. Therefore the bedroom switch controls the kitchen light. Per clue 2, the dining room switch doesn't control the dining room light (since the dining room is downstairs), which leaves the bathroom as the only switch that can control the light in the same room. The remaining switches and lights can be paired by elimination.

16 Secret Message 2

The message is FROM OXNARD TO MOAB, indicating the spy's itinerary as he relocated from California to Utah.

	a	b	c	d
1	FR	OR	NO	FM
2	AO	RX	NX	AB
3	MR	DR	OT	MO
4	MO	DO	AN	BO

We'll label the rows and columns for convenience. Note that the set of squares (3a, 3b, 4a, 4b) contains four letters twice each, and has two possible orientations: (M, R, O, D) and (R, D, M, O). Since either 4a or 4b must be O, we can eliminate O from 4d. Placing a B in that square forces 2d to be A, which then forces 2a to be O, and, continuing from there, we can place the rest of the letters by elimination.

26 The Crushed Cactus

Gravel crushed the cactus. The first step is to determine what order the siblings might be standing in. (We'll refer to them by their initials for convenience.) S, M, and E stand left to right in that order, in positions yet to be determined. J is at least three places from G, and isn't next to E. If G were to J's left, J would be forced to stand next to E, so J is to G's left, which gives us three possible lineups: JSMGE, JSMEG, and SJMEG. Let's examine the four statements and how they apply to each of those arrangements. As a reminder, those are as follows—E: someone next to me; M: someone at one end of the row; J: the person to my right; S: the person two to my right. The grid below shows who those statements are referring to if they are true.

	JSMGE	JSMEG	SJMEG
E	G	MG	MG
M	JE	JG	SG
J	S	S	M
S	G	E	M

Exactly two siblings are lying, so two are telling the truth, and the culprit must appear in exactly two statements. In each case, only G appears exactly twice, so although we don't know exactly how the children were standing, we know that G is the guilty sibling.

19 Digital Deletions 4

$$\begin{array}{r} 3\ 8\ 6 \\ +\ 3\ 7\ 8 \\ \hline 7\ 6\ 4 \\ -\ 5\ 7\ 8 \\ \hline 1\ 8\ 6 \end{array}$$

$$\begin{array}{r} 3\ 8 \\ +\ 3\ 8 \\ \hline 7\ 6 \\ -\ 5\ 8 \\ \hline 1\ 8 \end{array}$$

$$\begin{array}{r} 3 \\ +\ 3 \\ \hline 6 \\ -\ 5 \\ \hline 1 \end{array}$$

18 Card Sharp 2

From clue 5, the club and diamond can take values (C, D) as follows: (11, 1), (10, 2), ..., (1, 11). However, clue 2 restricts the values (C, D, S) to (11, 1, 7), (10, 2, 8), (9, 3, 9), ..., (5, 7, 13). Considering the four of hearts and clue 4, the possible combinations for (C, D, S, H) are reduced to (9, 3, 9, 4), (8, 4, 10, 4), (6, 6, 12, 4). Per clue 4, the two identical cards must be adjacent. For (9, 3, 9, 4), the two nines would have to be the third and fourth cards, but per clue 3, the fourth card is a seven or lower, so that combination is eliminated. For (8, 4, 10, 4), the second four would be in one of the two positions next to the face-up four of hearts. In either case one of the two remaining cards would be placed fourth, and both have a value equal to or higher than 8, so that's also impossible, leaving us with (6, 6, 12, 4). The two sixes are third and fourth, and they total 12, so they are the diamond and club (in that order, so the club is at the end of the row). That leaves the queen of spades in the first position.

20 Crazy Cars

Earwig dented Officer Nab's Cadillac. The following table shows the possible culprits for each statement, depending on whether those statements are true or false.

	True	False
A	CDEG	ABFH
B	ADEH	BCFG
C	BCEF	ADGH
D	BGH	ACDEF

The only one to appear in a single false statement (or, looked at another way, exactly three true statements) is Earwig.

74

42 Cafeteria Caper

The order was Dribble (who lied), Agatha, Catweed, Ethel, and Benny.

We know there is exactly one false statement. Consider Agatha and Dribble's statements. If they are both true, there is only one possible arrangement of Agatha, Catweed and Dribble: D – C A. In that case Benny's statement must be false (there isn't anywhere to place Benny and Ethel consecutively), and Ethel's statement must also be false (as there are only five positions). That's impossible, so either Agatha or Dribble's statement must be the false one, and Benny and Ethel's statements are both true.

From Benny and Ethel's statements, there are two possible arrangements of Agatha, Benny, and Ethel: A B E and A – E B. If Agatha lied and Dribble's statement is true, we can narrow down the arrangement to A B E D, but we cannot determine whether the full order is C A B E D or A B E D C. Since the vice principal was able to determine the students' order, Agatha can't be the liar. So Dribble lied and Agatha told the truth, which means the order must be D A C E B.

15 The Ticket Office

From front to back: Bert, Ethel, Christopher, Felicity, Doris, and Andy. There are only four ways that three men and three women can be arranged in a line so that no two men are adjacent: WMWMWM, MWWMWM, MWMWWM, or MWMWMW. From clue 1, there are three possible orders for the men, from front to back: CBA, CAB, or BCA. In all four arrangements of men and women, the last man and last woman are adjacent, and either A or B is the last man. According to clue 4, F is not next to A or B, so F cannot be the last woman in line. But F is behind E, per clue 2, so the order of women in EFD. Since F and E aren't adjacent, we can eliminate MWWMWM as an option. Per clue 4, F cannot be next to more than one man (who must be C). In the arrangements WMWMWM and MWMWMW, the second woman in line (who is F) is next to two men, so those arrangements are impossible, leaving MWMWWM as the only remaining option. The second man in line must be C (since he's next to F), which means the order of men is BCA, and we now know everyone's placement.

17 The Greatest Composer

	First name	Last name	Masterpiece
1	Loudhair	Moatsboat	*Ride of the Valley Girl*
2	George	Fishoven	*Miss Iowa*
3	Foxgang	Houndel	*Mood Lighting Sonata*
4	Ricky	Waggler	*The Magic Fruit*

Per clues 1 and 5, Houndel is not second and George is not third. That leaves only one position that fulfills clue 4: George in 2 and Houndel in 3. Loudhair isn't third either (per clue 5), which leaves Ricky as the only name in that column that can be correctly placed, so Ricky is in 4. Since Loudhair isn't in 3, he's in 1 and Foxgang is in 3. Per clue 2, *Mood Lighting Sonata* is one place above Waggler. It's not first (per clue 3), and it can't be second (since Houndel is already placed in 3), so it's correctly placed in 3 and Waggler is correctly placed in 4. *The Magic Fruit* can't also be correctly placed in 2, and it isn't first (per clue 3), so it's in 4. Bearing in mind that no remaining items are correctly placed, everything else can be placed by elimination.

19 Paper Trial

There are 12 possible routes, as shown below.

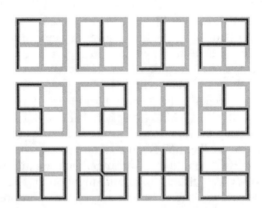

25 The Logical Library

The correct order is *Eerie Espionage*, *Fractious Friends*, *Awful Aunties*, *Creepy Cottages*, *Boring Baking*, *Ghoulish Games*, *Desperate Dating*.

We'll refer to the titles by their initial letters for convenience. From clues 2 and 5, possible arrangements are F??BG, F???GB, and FB??G (and their reflections), in some position. Let's refer to "A or E" as X and "C or D" as Y. From clues 3 and 4, X?X and Y??Y must also fit into the arrangment. That gives us these possibilities: XFXYBGY, YFXYXGB, and YFBYXGX. We can eliminate all of those arrangements' reflections, since reflecting them would place F in the sixth position, and per clue 1, no title is in the correct alphabetic position. Continuing to bear clue 1 in mind, we end up with these three possibilities: EFACBGD, DFECAGB, and DFBCAGE. In two of these three, A is to the right of D. But Mr. Prim told Miss Take that if he told her whether A was to the right or left of D, she would be able to determine the final arrangement. If A were to the right of D, knowing that fact would still leave the final arrangement of books ambiguous. Therefore A must be to the left of D, which leaves only one option, EFACBGD.

26 Digital Deletions 5

$$
\begin{array}{r}
7\ 9\ 6 \\
-\ 4\ 6\ 8 \\
\hline
3\ 2\ 8 \\
+\ 5\ 6\ 9 \\
\hline
8\ 9\ 7
\end{array}
\qquad
\begin{array}{r}
7\ 6 \\
-\ 4\ 8 \\
\hline
2\ 8 \\
+\ 5\ 9 \\
\hline
8\ 7
\end{array}
\qquad
\begin{array}{r}
6 \\
-\ 4 \\
\hline
2 \\
+\ 5 \\
\hline
7
\end{array}
$$

32 Gullible Garage

Mr. Squidge can expect his car on Friday. The family has four members, and at least one tells the truth, but there are more liars in the family than truth-tellers. There must therefore be three liars and one truth-teller among the four. The correct day, then, is the one that appears in exactly one statement: Friday. (And Aaron is the truth-teller.)

29 Lousy Electrics 2

The bathroom switch controls the bedroom light; the bedroom switch controls the bathroom light; the den switch controls the kitchen light; the dining room switch controls the dining room light; the kitchen switch controls the den light; and the living room switch controls the living room light.

After entering the information from the clues into the grid, we have this:

light fixtures

	bathroom	bedroom	den	dining room	kitchen	living room
bathroom	✕				✕	✕
bedroom		✕	✕	✕	✕	
den		✕				✕
dining room	✕	✕				✕
kitchen	✕	✕		✕	✕	
living room	✕		✕		✕	

switches

We are given that the light switches in exactly two of the six rooms control the light in the same room. The only switches those could be are the ones in the den, dining room, and living room. The kitchen switch controls either the den or living room light, so one of those lights is not controlled by the switch in its own room, which means the dining room switch must control the dining room light. That means, by elimination, the kitchen light must be controlled by the den switch, and so the living room light must be the other light controlled by the switch in the same room. Everything else can be paired by elimination.

36 False Filasteins

Earwig is the dean. The table at the top of the next page shows the possible candidates for the dean, depending on whether those statements are true or false.

	True	False
A	BCFH	ADEG
B	BH	ACDEFG
C	BDEH	ACFG
D	CFH	ABDEG

Since three professors are lying, the dean must appear three times in the "False" column (or, to look at it another way, only once in the "True" column). Two names fit that description: Dibdib and Earwig. If Dibdib is the dean, though, he must be one of the liars, which is impossible, so Earwig (who makes no statement at all) is the dean.

40 Lunches and Lies

Gripe pays the bill. The following table shows the possible paying patrons for each statement, depending on whether those statements are true or false.

	True	False
A	CEH	ABDFG
B	AFGH	BCDE
C	BCGH	ADEF
D	ABC	DEFGH

Since two statements are lies, the bill-payer must appear twice on the "True" side of the table and twice on the "False" side. Exactly three diners do so: Antwit, Babble, and Gripe. If the bill-payer were Antwit, though, Antwit's statement would be a lie; likewise for Babble's statement if Babble were the bill-payer. Since the diner who paid did not tell a lie, it therefore can't be either of those two and must be Gripe, who made no statement at all.

28 Screen Test

	First name	Last name	1st word of film title	2nd word of film title
1	Meryl	Hopeburn	*National*	*Motel*
2	Elizabeth	Garbanzo	*Sofa*	*Holiday*
3	Audrey	Stripe	*Grand*	*Velour*
4	Greta	Dressmaker	*Romaine*	*Choice*

Per clues 5 and 6, *National* is not in position 4 and *Grand* is not in position 1. If *National* were in 3, there would be no position for *Grand* that wasn't adjacent to it, contradicting clue 1; if *Grand* were in 2, a similar contradiction arises. Therefore *National* is in 1 or 2 and *Grand* is in 3 or 4. Together, they can't be in 1 and 4 or it would be impossible for any first words to be correctly placed, so either *National* is correct in 2 or *Grand* is correct in 3. Let's assume the first of those possibilities is the case; then Elizabeth is in 3 (per clue 5), Grand is in 4 (per clue 1), and Garbanzo is correctly placed in 3 (per clue 6). Then where can Dressmaker go? Not in 1 (since *Velour* is above it, per clue 2), nor in 2 (since that would make two correctly placed surnames), nor in 4 with *Grand* (which would contradict clue 4). This arrangement, then, can't be correct, and instead we have *National* in 1, Elizabeth correctly placed in 2, Garbanzo in 2, and *Grand* correctly placed in 3. Audrey is one place above *Choice* (clue 3), but can't also be correctly placed in 1, so Audrey is in 3 and *Choice* is correctly placed in 4. *Velour* is one place above Dressmaker (clue 2), but isn't in 1 (since Garbanzo is already placed in 2), or correctly placed in 2 (since *Choice* is already correctly placed), so *Velour* is in 3 and Dressmaker is in 4. The only surname that can possibly be correctly placed is Hopeburn in 1. Given that nothing else can be correctly positioned, everything else can be placed by elimination.

39 Lousy Electrics 3

The bathroom switch controls the kitchen light; the bedroom switch controls the den light; the den switch controls the dining room light; the dining room switch controls the bedroom light; the kitchen switch controls the bathroom light; and the living room switch controls the living room light.

From clues 2 and 5, the den light is the only one that could be controlled by the bedroom switch, and from clues 1 and 5, only the den switch could be the one that controls the dining room light. After entering those pairings into the grid (eliminating other options for the den light and den switch), as well as the rest of the information from the clues, we have this:

light fixtures

	bathroom	bedroom	den	dining room	kitchen	living room
bathroom		×	×	×		
bedroom	×	×	O	×	×	×
den	×	×	×	O	×	×
dining room			×	×		
kitchen		×	×	×		×
living room	×	×	×	×		

switches

We can see now that the bedroom light can only be controlled by the dining room switch, which leaves two options for the bathroom light: the bathroom switch or the kitchen switch. But if the bathroom switch controls the bathroom light, the only option left for the kitchen switch is the kitchen light, and only one switch controls the light in the same room. Therefore the kitchen switch must be the one that controls the bathroom light. That leaves only the living room switch as the one that can be controlling the correct light, so it controls the living room light, and by elimination the bathroom switch controls the kitchen light.

32 Digital Deletions 6

$$
\begin{array}{r} 4\ 9\ 5 \\ +\ 3\ 7\ 8 \\ \hline 8\ 7\ 3 \\ -\ 4\ 7\ 8 \\ \hline 3\ 9\ 5 \end{array}
\qquad
\begin{array}{r} 4\ 9 \\ +\ 3\ 8 \\ \hline 8\ 7 \\ -\ 4\ 8 \\ \hline 3\ 9 \end{array}
\qquad
\begin{array}{r} 4 \\ +\ 3 \\ \hline 7 \\ -\ 4 \\ \hline 3 \end{array}
$$

34 **Moving Picture 2**

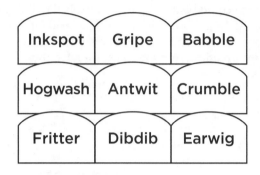

Inkspot	Gripe	Babble
Hogwash	Antwit	Crumble
Fritter	Dibdib	Earwig

For convenience, let the statement "only one remains in the same row, and only one remains in the same column" be denoted by "X." From clue 2, Earwig is somewhere in the column immediately to Dibdib's right. Dibdib can't be in the left column with Earwig in the middle column (violates X), so Dibdib is in the center column and Earwig is in the right column. Per clues 5 and 6, Babble is in the top row, Hogwash is in the middle row, and Dibdib is in the bottom row (and can be placed in the middle seat of that row). Since Babble has stayed in the same row, no one else is seated in their original row. Crumble is somewhere to Dibdib's right (clue 4), but not in the top row (violates X), so Crumble is in the rightmost seat in the middle or bottom row, and is the person who stayed in the same column. Per clue 1, Antwit is above Earwig, but isn't in the top row (violates X), so Antwit is in the middle row, Earwig is in the bottom row of the right column, and Crumble is in the middle row of the right column. Inkspot is somewhere to Antwit's left (clue 3), so Antwit isn't in the left column, and the rightmost seat in Antwit's row is occupied by Crumble, so Antwit is in the middle seat of the middle row, and Inkspot is in the left column. We know Hogwash is in the middle row, and only the leftmost seat in that row isn't yet accounted for, so Hogwash is seated there. Inkspot isn't in the bottom row (violates X), so must be in the leftmost seat of the top row. Babble isn't in the middle column (violates X) and is therefore in the rightmost seat of the top row. Per X, Gripe must have changed rows and columns, so Gripe moved to the middle seat of the top row, and by elimination Fritter is in the leftmost seat of the bottom row.

49 Lies and Legerdemain

The white cup has four balls under it, the gray cup has two, and the black cup has three.

The order in which the balls are moved is irrelevant. In total, one ball is removed from under each cup. At most two of those three can be placed under the white cup, at most two can be placed under the gray, and up to three can be placed under the black.

Assume clue 2 is true; in that case, two balls (the maximum) must have been placed under the gray cup. That leaves two balls each under the white and black cups, and one ball as yet unaccounted for. Since that's only five balls in total, it's impossible for clue 3 to be true. And since the gray cup has four balls under it and the black cup has at least two, it's also impossible for clue 1 to be true. That would make two false statements, which is one too many. Therefore clue 2 must be the false statement.

Per clue 3, the number of balls under the white and black cups must be at least seven. The two balls under each cup and the three that are still to be placed account for all seven of those, so no balls are placed under the gray cup, and it ends up with two balls underneath it. At most two balls can go under the white cup, so at least one must go under the black cup. But per clue 1, the total number of balls under the gray and black cups is at most five, so only one ball is placed under the black cup (leaving a total of three) and the other two balls are placed under the white cup (leaving a total of four).

37 Digital Deletions 7

```
  4 3 8        3 8         3
+ 1 5 6      + 1 6       + 1
-------      -----       ---
  5 9 4        5 4         4
- 2 6 5      - 2 5       - 2
-------      -----       ---
  3 2 9        2 9         2
+ 5 3 8      + 5 8       + 5
-------      -----       ---
  8 6 7        8 7         7
```

43 Costume Competition

	First name	Last name	Town	Costume
1	Gordon	Mop	Arcata	robot
2	Andrea	Bottle	Pella	witch
3	Edith	Haggis	Tumwater	penguin
4	Cuthbert	Whinge	Jackson	carrot

Per clue 3, the robot costume must be in position 1 or 2. If it's correct in 2, then Tumwater is correct in 4. But then consider clue 1; the penguin costume can be in 3 or 4. It can't also be correct in 3, but if it's in 4, then Pella is also correct in 3. Since all possibilities lead to contradictions, the robot costume must instead be in 1, with Bottle in 2 and Tumwater in 3. With Tumwater now occupying position 3, there's only one way to place the items in clue 1: Gordon in 1, Pella in 2, and the penguin costume correctly placed in 3. And with Bottle in 2, there's only one way to place the items in clue 2: Mop in 1 and Edith correctly placed in 3. There is now only one possible last name and town that can be correctly placed: Whinge in 4 and Arcata in 1. Given that nothing else can be correctly positioned, everything else can be placed by elimination.

50 The Solar Society 3

initial arrangement

final arrangement

The initial arrangement was: Ms. Neptune in chair 1, Mr. Jupiter in chair 2, Mr. Uranus in chair 3, Ms. Venus in chair 4, Mr. Saturn in chair 5, and Mr. Mercury in chair 6. The final arrangement was: Mr. Saturn in chair 1, Ms. Neptune in chair 2, Mr. Uranus in chair 3, Mr. Mercury in chair 4, Mr. Jupiter in chair 5, and Ms. Venus in chair 6.

Let's consider Neptune and Jupiter's positions. Per clues 1 and 3, Jupiter moved to the opposite seat (or, to think of it another way, moved three seats clockwise) and Neptune moved one seat clockwise. Furthermore, they did not end up in adjacent seats. There are only two possible ways they could be arranged with those constraints (in some orientation): J???N? moving to ???J?N, or J????N moving to N??J?? (the other three possible starting seats for N result in a seat next to J, or in sharing a seat with J, which is impossible).

Now let's consider clues 4 and 5. Mercury and Venus exchange positions, and Uranus doesn't move. This means that, between them, they occupy the same three seats at the end that they started in. This means that their three seats can never be occupied by Neptune or Jupiter. Let's look again at the two possible arrangments for Neptune and Jupiter, but combining the starting and ending positions for each, and placing an X in any seat that's occupied in either position. That gives us X??XXX and X??X?X. The first of the two is impossible, as it only leaves two seats unused for Mercury, Venus, and Uranus. In the second position, only two of the unused seats are two positions apart, so (per clue 4) Mercury and Venus sat in them in some order, and Uranus sat in the other one. Saturn was seated in the leftover chair in each arrangement. This gives us the following initial and final arrangements (we'll refer to Mercury and Venus as A and B for now, and determine which is which later): JUASBN and NUBJAS. Per clue 5, Uranus is sitting in chair 3 or 5. If he is in chair 5, though, then in the initial position, A was seated in chair 6 and B was in chair 2. Both of those chairs are next to chair 1, and since Venus is A or B, this contradicts clue 2. Uranus must therefore be in chair 3 (which fixes the final orientation), with A starting in chair 4 and B in chair 6. Since Venus isn't next to chair 1, Venus is A and Mercury is B, and everyone's placement is now determined.

52 Disordered Dogs

	First name	Last name	Age (in years)	Color
1	Woofgang	Doo	8	orange
2	Droolius	Wipes	4	blue
3	Poodle	Bones	3	yellow
4	Mary	Amadaypuss	5	red
5	Chewbee	Puppins	7	green
6	Sherlock	Caesar	6	white

First, compare clues 3 and 4. The 3- and 4-year-old dogs must each be in position 1, 2, or 3. If the 3-year-old dog is correct in position 1 (with Sherlock in 4), where can the 4-year-old dog be? Not in 2 (since Mary would then be in 4, where Sherlock already is) and not in 3 either (since that would make two correct items in the age column). So we can eliminate that option. What if the 3-year-old is in position 2, with Sherlock correct in 5? Then the 4-year-old can't be in position 1 (since that would place Mary in 3, making two correct items in the first name column), and can't be in position 3 either (since Sherlock is once again in the position where Mary would go). That only leaves position 3 for the 3-year-old, and so the dog in red is correctly positioned in 4 and Sherlock is in 6. The 4-year-old, then, is in 1 or 2, Mary is in 3 or 4, and Puppins is in 4 or 5.

Now let's look at clue 5. The dog in yellow, the 5-year-old, and Chewbee are in consecutive positions, which can only be 1, 2, and 3 or 3, 4, and 5, based on the empty positions available. If they are in 1, 2, and 3 respectively, then Mary could not also be in 3 and would be in 4, but then the 4-year-old would have to be in 2, where we had just placed the 5-year-old, which is impossible. The dog in yellow, then, is in 3, the 5-year-old is in 4, and Chewbee is in 5.

How about clue 6? The dog in blue can't be correctly placed in 1 (since red is already correctly placed in 4), so the only place left that it can fit is 2, with Amadaypuss in 4. That forces Puppins to be in 5, which puts Mary in 4 and the 4-year-old in 2.

Of the first names, the only one left that could be correctly placed is Droolius in position 2. That only leaves 1 and 3 still unaccounted for. Per clue 2, Poodle must be in 3. The dog in orange, then, can only be in 1, and Caesar must be in 6. That leaves Doo as the only last name that can be correctly placed, in position 1. As for the ages, only the 7-year-old can be correctly placed, in position 5. The 8-year-old can't be in position 6 because then it wouldn't be next to Wipes (clue 1), so it's in 1, and Wipes is in 2. The dog in white can't be correctly placed in 5, so it's in 6. Everything else is placed by elimination.

56 Pentomime

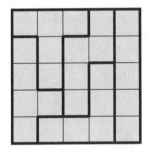 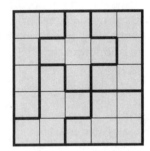

42 Digital Deletions 8

```
   3 1 4        3 4          4
 + 2 4 9      + 2 9        + 2
 ───────      ─────        ───
   5 6 3        6 3          6
 - 4 1 5      - 4 5        - 5
 ───────      ─────        ───
   1 4 8        1 8          1
 + 2 1 4      + 1 4        + 1
 ───────      ─────        ───
   3 6 2        3 2          2
```

54 Lousy Electrics 4

The bathroom switch controls the library light; the bedroom switch controls the den light; the den switch controls the dining room light; the dining room switch controls the bedroom light; the kitchen switch controls the kitchen light; the library switch controls the bathroom light, and the living room switch controls the living room light.

From clues 3, 4, and 6, the den switch can only control the dining room light. From clues 2 and 6 (and the dining room light already being accounted for), the bedroom switch can only control the den light. From clues 1, 2, and 5 (and the dining room and den lights already being accounted for), the dining room switch can only control the bedroom light. After entering those pairings into the grid (eliminating other options for the bedroom, den, and dining room lights), as well as the rest of the information from the clues, we have this:

light fixtures

	bathroom	bedroom	den	dining room	kitchen	library	living room
bathroom		X	X	X	X		
bedroom	X	X	O	X	X	X	X
den	X	X	X	O	X	X	X
dining room	X	O	X	X	X	X	X
kitchen		X	X	X		X	X
library		X	X	X			X
living room	X	X	X	X			

switches

There are two lights that the kitchen switch might control. Let's assume it controls the bathroom light. In that case, neither the bathroom nor kitchen switch is one that controls the light in the same room, so the library and living room switches must be those two switches. But then that eliminates every light that the bathroom switch could control, so that's impossible, and the kitchen switch must control the kitchen light.

If the bathroom light is controlled by the bathroom switch, then by elimination, the living room light must be controlled by the living room switch and the library light by the library switch. That makes four switches controlling lights in the same room, which is impossible, so the bathroom light is controlled by the only remaining option, the library switch. That leaves the bathroom and living room switches, and the library and living room lights. One switch must still control the light in the same room, so that's the living room, and the bathroom switch controls the library light.

36 Card Sharp 3

From clue 5, the second and fourth cards must be face cards, so the only card that isn't a face card is the third one. Since the spade isn't adjacent to a face card (clue 2), it must be the fourth card, which is only adjacent to the third card. That leaves the heart and club as the center two cards in some order. Those two cards total 20 (clue 3) and include a face card, so their values are either (7, 13), (8, 12), or (9, 11) in some order. None of those values can be added to the king of diamond's value of 13 to make 18, so it's the two black cards that total 18 (clue 4). The spade is a face card, so its value is at least that of a jack, 11. The smallest possible values, then, of the club and spade are 7 and 11, and since those total 18, those values are correct. Since we've now identified the 7 of clubs as the sole non-face card, it's the third card, and the second card must be the king of hearts (whose value totals 20 when added to the 7, per clue 3).

55 The Solar Society 4

initial arrangement   final arrangement

The initial arrangement was: Ms. Venus in chair 1, Ms. Saturn in chair 2, Mr. Uranus in chair 3, Mr. Mercury in chair 4, Ms. Earth in chair 5, Mr. Jupiter in chair 6, Mr. Pluto in chair 7, and Ms. Neptune in chair 8. The final arrangement was: Mr. Mercury in chair 1, Ms. Venus in chair 2, Mr. Jupiter in chair 3, Ms. Neptune in chair 4, Mr. Pluto in chair 5, Mr. Uranus in chair 6, Ms. Earth in chair 7, and Ms. Saturn in chair 8.

Earth and Pluto swap positions (clue 1), as do Uranus and Jupiter (clue 5). That means the four of them always occupy the same set of four seats, and no one else ever sits in those seats. For now, let's refer to Earth and Pluto as A and B, and Uranus and Jupiter as X and Y; we'll determine which is which later. A and B are two places apart (clue 1), and X and Y are three places apart (clue 5). This gives us four possible positions for them (in some orientation): ?X?AYB??, ???AXB?Y, ?Y?A?BX?, and ??YA?B?X.

Venus moves one place clockwise (clue 4), but in the third and fourth arrangements above, the only seat she could start from is next to X, who is either Uranus or Jupiter, which contradicts clue 4, so those arrangements are impossible and we can focus on the first two options only. Mercury moves three places counterclockwise (clue 2); there's only one way he can do that in those two arrangements, which in each case leaves only one way for Neptune to move to the opposite seat (clue 3). Those arrangements are ?XMAYBN? moving to ?YNBXA?M, and ?M?AXBNY moving to ??NBYAMX.

Venus moves one place clockwise (clue 4), which she could do in either of those arrangements, from the starting position ?XMAYBNV or VM?AXBNY. However, we have already shown that Venus can't start out seated next to X or Y (per clue 4), and she's next to Y in the second of those options (remember, they are sitting in a circle). So the first option is the only possibility, and the remaining seat is filled by Saturn, giving us SXMAYBNV moving to VYNBXASM.

Now let's figure out which is which for A, B, X, and Y. Per clue 6, Pluto (who is either A or B) sits closer in the final arrangement to Uranus than to Jupiter (who are X and Y in some order). Both A and B are closer to X than to Y, so Uranus is X and Jupiter is Y. Pluto's seat in the final arrangement is chair 5 and neither Uranus nor Jupiter is the group leader (clue 6). If Pluto were A, the chair four seats away from A's ending position would be chair 1, which would mean that Uranus (X) was seated in chair 1 in the original position. But that would make Uranus the group leader, contradicting clue 6. So Pluto is B, Earth is A, and since we know Pluto's final position is chair 5, everyone's placement is now determined.

46 Card Sharp 4

Two face-down cards total 20 (clue 2); those cards could be a king and a 7, a queen and an 8, a jack and a 9, or two 10s. One of those cards must be one of the three rightmost cards that together total 13 (clue 4); say it's the lowest possible card, a 7. That card and the 5 of spades add up to 12. That's the most those cards can total without the set of three cards going above 13, so the two cards that total 20 are a king and a 7, and the other face-down card is an ace. That king is the only face card among the face-down cards, so it's a heart (clue 3), and it's the second card (since it isn't one of the cards in clue 4). The 7 isn't a heart (clue 2), so the other heart (clue 3) is the ace, which can't be next to the king (clue 1), so it's the fifth card. The third card is the 7, and since all four suits appear (clue 1), it's the 7 of clubs.

47 Football Falsehoods

Hogwash pays for the tickets. The following table shows who each statement refers to, depending on whether those statements are true or false.

	True	False
C	BEH	ACDFG
E	BCEFG	ADH
F	BDE	ACFGH
G	ACEFH	BDG

Since two are lying, the one buying the tickets must appear twice in the "False" column (or, to look at it another way, twice in the "True" column). Three names fit that description: Crumble, Fritter, and Hogwash. But for Crumble or Fritter to be the ticket-buyer, they would have to be lying, which is impossible, so Hogwash (who makes no statement at all) buys them.

57 The Mind-Stretcher

It is possible to find out whether or not a statement X is true irrespective of whether a truth-teller or liar is responding and without knowing which word means "yes." Once you can do that, all that is needed is a technique for narrowing down the possible days by asking questions about decreasing parts of the week. A good opening question on Day 1 would be: "Are you the kind of guard who would say that exactly one of the following two statements is true: 'Today is Sunday, Monday, Tuesday, or Wednesday' and 'Ho means yes'?"

If the current day is indeed Sunday, Monday, Tuesday, or Wednesday, then it does not matter whether the guard is a truth-teller or a liar, or which word means "yes"; the answer will always be "mo." Let's examine the options. If "ho" means "yes", then both statements are true. A truth-teller would not say that exactly one of the statements is true, and "mo" means "no," so the truthful guard would answer "mo"; a liar would say exactly one statement was true (since that's false), but will lie and deny they are the sort of guard who would say that, and since "mo" means "no," the lying guard will also answer "mo." If, rather, "ho" means "no," then exactly one statement is true and the foregoing situations are reversed; a truthful guard and a lying guard will both answer the question "yes," and since "ho" means "no," they will both say "mo."

In the case that it is not Sunday, Monday, Tuesday, or Wednesday, a similar analysis will reveal that the guard (whether truthful or lying, and whatever the meanings of "ho" and "mo") will always answer "ho."

The prisoner can continue to use this question structure on the next two days to narrow down the possible days of the week. For instance, if the first answer was "mo," the prisoner could then ask, "Are you the kind of guard who would say that only one of the following two statements is true: 'Yesterday was Sunday or Monday' and 'Ho means yes'?" If the answer to that is "ho" (indicating that yesterday was not Sunday or Monday), then the final question could be "Are you the kind of guard who would say that only one of the following two statements is true: 'Two days ago it was Tuesday' and 'Ho means yes'?" The answer to that will reveal which day it was, which will make it clear what day it is currently. Three questions is the maximum that will be needed, though it's possible to find the correct day in two questions with some luck, if the correct day is on the smaller side of a 4–3 division, and then again on the smaller side of a 2–1 division.

48 Digital Deletions 9

$$
\begin{array}{r}
8\ 4\ 6 \\
-\ 5\ 6\ 8 \\
\hline
2\ 7\ 8 \\
+\ 4\ 5\ 3 \\
\hline
7\ 3\ 1 \\
-\ 5\ 6\ 4 \\
\hline
1\ 6\ 7
\end{array}
\qquad
\begin{array}{r}
8\ 4 \\
-\ 5\ 6 \\
\hline
2\ 8 \\
+\ 4\ 5 \\
\hline
7\ 3 \\
-\ 5\ 6 \\
\hline
1\ 7
\end{array}
\qquad
\begin{array}{r}
8 \\
-\ 6 \\
\hline
2 \\
+\ 5 \\
\hline
7 \\
-\ 6 \\
\hline
1
\end{array}
$$

12 **Presto!**

The order that the rabbit occupies the hats is C, D, B, A. Each elf says the rabbit is in one of two hats; in order, those pairs are BC, AD, BD, and AC. Since the rabbit visits each hat exactly once, this gives us two possible orders: BADC and CDBA. However, in the first case, all four locations are adjacent to the elf who was speaking (which were in A, B, C, and D, in order). The second order is therefore correct.

24 **Shifting Shapes**

A: increasing the number of sides; B: drilling holes; C: painting gray; D: painting white; E: rotating 90° counterclockwise; F: increasing the number of sides; G: rotating 90° counterclockwise; H: painting gray; I: filling in holes.

6 **Four Aces**

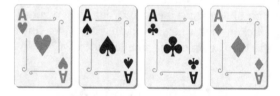

There are six possible positions for the spade and club in which the spade is to the club's left: SC??, ?SC?, ??SC, S?C?, ?S?C, and S??C. We can immediately eliminate the three in which the two unknown cards are adjacent since, per clue 3, the diamond and heart are not adjacent. Of the remaining three, S?C? and ?S?C both contradict clue 2; in the first, it would be impossible for any card to be in its original position (since the spade and club are, together, occupying the original positions of the heart and diamond), and in the second, both the spade and club are in their original positions. So ?SC? is the correct position, with the spade in its original position and the other cards can now be placed by elimination.

53 The School of Logic

Charge is the best candidate, and Electron is (very probably) telling the truth.

We'll refer to the candidates by their initials for convenience. Analyzing the first four statements, we soon see that whether the speaker is a truth-teller or a liar, they will always give the same answer. For instance, if A is a truth-teller, A's answer will be "yes" if A or D is the best candidate (since the first statement is false and the second is true) and "no" if B, C, or E is the best candidate (since both statements are false). But if A is a liar, A's answer will still be "yes" if A or D is the best candidate (since both statements are true, so A will lie and say "yes") and "no" if B, C, or E is the best candidate (since the first statement is true and the second is false, so A will lie and say "no").

We can therefore construct a table to show which groups are indicated to contain the best candidate for each "yes" and "no" answer:

	yes	no
A	AD	BCE
B	AC	BDE
C	AC	BDE
D	ACE	BD

Two of the five candidates (including E) answered "no," so the best candidate must appear in the "no" column at least once but no more than twice. A only appears in the "yes" column, and B, D, and E appear in the "no" column three times, so C must be the best candidate, and A and E are the two candidates who answered "no." Since E was present for all the questions, E would have been able to determine that there was enough information in the other candidates' answers to reveal that E was not the best candidate for the job, and since E wanted the job very badly (as they all did), it is very likely that E was not, in fact, happy just then.

48 Digital Deletions 10

```
    2 4 9       2 9       2
  + 4 3 6     + 3 6     + 3
  ───────     ─────     ───
    6 8 5       6 5       5
  − 3 5 8     − 3 8     − 3
  ───────     ─────     ───
    3 2 7       2 7       2
  + 4 1 9     + 4 9     + 4
  ───────     ─────     ───
    7 4 6       7 6       6
```

About the Author

Barry R. Clarke writes enigmas for *The Daily Telegraph* and *Prospect* magazine. His puzzle work has also appeared on BBC television. He has published papers on quantum mechanics and an academic treatise *The Quantum Puzzle: A Critique of Quantum Physics and Electrodynamics*. His Ph.D. in Shakespeare authorship  studies has also led to the scholarly work *Francis Bacon's Contribution to Shakespeare: A New Attribution Method*.

He has won awards as a short-film maker, drawn cartoons for some of his puzzle books, and written comedy sketches for the BBC and ITV. Being also a talented guitarist, he has one unfulfilled ambition, and that is to record an album of his own music. He is inspired by the work of Albert Einstein, Jimi Hendrix, Audrey Hepburn, Immanuel Kant, and Laurel and Hardy!